How to Succeed in Life?

Joginder Singh
Former Director, CBI

DIAMOND BOOKS

Publisher : **Diamond Pocket Books (P) Ltd.**
X-30, Okhla Industrial Area, Phase-II
New Delhi-110020
Phone : 011-40712200
E-mail : wecare@diamondbooks.in
Website : www.diamondbooks.in
Edition : 2025
Printed by : Adarsh Printers, Delhi- 110032

How To Succeed In Life?
By - *Joginder Singh, Former Director, CBI*

Dedication

This book is dedicated to my grandchildren, Daanis, Mannat, Amrita, Ruhani and Meher.

Preface

There are different kinds of books on the subject of self improvement. This is one of them, but vastly different in more than one sense. It not only states the obvious, but brings home, the fact, that by following a few simple tips, you can literally make what you want in your life. While in a way, we all want success, but most of the time, we are not clear about our aim. Whenever I have questioned a few young friends, their standard reply is to get a good job. But what that job, should be, they are hazy and ambiguous. Success has many components. This book deals with them and how by mastering them, in simple and precise language, you can attain your goals. Failure in any venture is a natural way, to discover, as to where you could have gone wrong and in a way, it is the best teacher. There is a price tag on everything in life, including our achievements, in any given field. But the problem is that we want success, without paying its price. The price is generally in the form of hard work and denial of immediate gratification, for a long term realisation of your ambition. In other words, it means keeping on working, and never, ever giving up, till you have reached your goal. Thanks to the suggestions of my good friend and Publisher, Sh. Narendar Kumar, the chapters of this book, have been so written, that even if you get ten minutes, waiting in between the meetings or catching a plane or a train, you can finish it. What we get out of this book is for each one of the readers to decide. It is a stand alone book, which you can read any where from any chapter or any page, and still find something suiting your need.

–Author

Contents

1

How To Manage Your Time, To Achieve Outstanding Results?

Time is one commodity, which is given, in an equal measure, to each human being. Some, by using it prudently and sensibly, reach great heights in business, industry or in their chosen sphere of work.

Some students by using the same twenty four hours intelligently make it to the top jobs, both in the Government and private sectors. Every body can reach the top, by following some of the rules suggested below. The list is only illustrative and not exhaustive. The best way to use time, is by planning in advance, on what you want to spend it on. However, care should be taken to spend your time, on what matters most to you.

If we fail to plan, then we are planning to fail. Using the instrument of planning, for proper time management, is not a waste of time.

I, on my part, list all the jobs, to be done for the day and sometimes, I go on noting them, as they occur to me, the previous evening or even in the midnight. I also ask, my Secretary, to note the engagements and tasks to be done, not only in his diary, but also on a calendar in my study. I have also programmed my computer to remind me as to what I have do. My email account sends me an email every day, as to what engagements, I have accepted and what more is to be done during the day.

While organising your life, work or time, do it in a right order, which makes sense to you, and which enhances your efficiency. Before starting my day, I personally like to remove clutter, both in my study, as well as, in my drawing room, where I work for half a day. Whatever you do, you must work, on pre-determined and set goals and spend time, in that direction. Above all, you must decide, as to what you want to attain in your profession or life . But make sure that your goals are specific, measurable, realistic and achievable. It is a perpetual question, to which we have to go on seeking answers on a continuous basis.

There are plenty of people, whose approach is, to take ,whatever life, brings to them. The result is, that such persons lead a jaded life. A purpose in life is nothing more than a destination, to which we want to reach at any or in a given time.

When I joined service, I did not even know, what heights I could achieve. My objective was, to do the best, for the present assigned job and make it a thundering success, with a positive approach. This approach won me appreciation and admiration. I was considered trustworthy for any work assigned to me.

One thing, we must all bear in mind is, that nobody is born perfect. We must learn from each other, including, from the mistakes and the secrets of success, of others. At the same time, we must make sure, that we live our life in alignment with our aspirations. The odds against achieving your purpose, may be high, but remember, that nothing is impossible. Do not live a half life, or be in the state of denial, in case you have a problem.

The best successes are not easy. They involve, a heavy cost, in the form of perseverance and efforts.

Our present life, is the result, of our own efforts. It is upto, each one of us, to mould or build, or improve upon it, as we want or like.

Whatever we are doing, or do, should be done, in the most effective and productive manner possible. This can be done only by efficient and constructive use of our time.

Our objective should be, to live our life in configuration with our goals, despite the constraints, which are bound, to come, in whatever we do. This is something to be done daily and not periodically. 80/ 20 is an excellent rule, propagated by an Italian Economist Pareto. It can be applied to our goals, as well as time management. It includes identifying , as to which 20% time utilised and goals achieved will give 80% achievement, fulfilment and happiness against the collective result of 100%. However, it need to be made certain, that 80/20 rule is in line with total and complete purpose or purposes in your life.

Not only the 80/20 is vital for our goals, but it is equally vital for deciding the 80/20 route, or path for management of time, we need to use it, for realising our ambitions.

There can be, more than one way, to attain our aim, or reach our destination. If we choose an approach, which involves, little effort, we choose a little reward route. Other routes, also include, despite our best and soaring efforts, reaping low rewards, apart from the path of high endeavour, and low rewards. Of course, higher exertion always means high rewards. There are some people, who with little effort can get high rewards.

Prioritising and having a Do List, is of the utmost importance. Keep on updating your do list and work according to your priorities. You can have a running DO List or a Day's List or Monthly List or Long Term goals List.

Whatever we might be doing, we must be prepared for the unexpected interruptions, which are a part of life. Pad your time and keep some time for unexpected disruptions. An unexpected visit from a close friend or a call from the spouse, or a wrong number, as an intrusion, is not strange.

We all have our best biological time, when we are at the peak of our efficiency. Some are morning persons, others are night owls. I am an afternoon person and start my work from 2 p.m., which can go on till 10 p.m. I shun all pre afternoon commitments. I use my best time, what I consider the highest priority work.

Nobody, except God, is perfect. I do my best for anything I do or have to do, and then forget after I have put in my most excellent effort. This is one approach, which is one of the best techniques of time management.

A part of excelling and good time management, is to do, the intelligent passing over, or neglecting, the trivial or the tasks, which do not have long term values either , by delegating to others or by forgetting them.

Another time management techniques, which gives the highest dividend is to say "NO', to time wasting activities, which do not contribute to the achievement of your goals. However, make certain that when you say "NO", it should be done politely and not rudely.

Go on asking yourself, constantly, about any activity you are engaged in, whether it is the most effective and productive use of your time. Constant introspection, helps us to remain focussed on our objectives.

Wise management of the time can add hours to our productivity. It is quite common, to waste hours together, in commuting to your place of work. It is possible to fit in a lesson or two or read some useful material even during the journey time. I, on my part, always select in advance, as to how I should spend such a time slot. If the journey is by plane or car, or train, I prefer to work on my lap top, for, either a chapter of my next book or an article. Even those, using the public transport, can always select a task, or have a sheet of paper relevant, to their job or studies ready for memorising or preparing themselves, for their next assignment or engagement.

Time by itself is nothing, unless it is or can be used, to better out lot, or station in life. We should use time as a tool, not a crutch.

Do not waste time on regret or lament for wasted time, as it is a still more wasted time. Start whatever you have to do, right now. ■■■

2

How to Use 80/20 Rule For Spectacular Results?

In our fast paced life, where we run, from one meeting to the other, or from one commitment to another, we forget, that life's basic purpose, is to enjoy it and live happily. It is not necessary that we should do everything ourselves.

Pareto principle enunciates that 80% results come from 20% efforts. However, when it comes to living our lives, we tend to overlook, this vital principle. By using this principle effectively, we can have, a good life and a good living. Incidentally, both are intertwined. We can apply , 80/20 to our career, relationships, health, habits, goal achievement, productivity, emotions, and in short to every pursuit.

However, this rule does not preclude delegation or doing more than our job. For instance, whenever I go out, I list all the works to be done, whether it is for marketing or for banking or for meeting. I apply this rule, even when I go for my morning exercise or even while even taking bath. I listen to my own positive thinking books on my digital recorders or cassette players, during those timings.

Of course, I do it unconsciously and mechanically, without even realizing that I am doing. I not only avoid, but get the non essential chores done from others, to save my time to focus on my priorities and goals. My Private Secretary and Driver are assigned the recurrent and ordinary work.

Simultaneously, I enjoy, what I like doing quality work. I also make a deliberate effort, to cut out negativity and keep company , only with the people I enjoy. Whatever we do, we must be clear about the destination, we want to reach or what we want to accomplish most and what matters most to us.

It will be best to list everything from the smallest to the biggest thing, we want to accomplish. Now identify which goals fit 80/20 rules. These are 20 % goals, which, when achieved, will give you 80% satisfaction or happiness. Many a time, it is worthwhile to examine, whether we are living our purpose or not.

Of course, our purposes vary depending upon our environment and the influences, to which we are exposed. Our answers to our aims and objectives are definitely inculcated in us, by our peers, parents and even our religious or non-religious upbringing.

However, if we are not living fully, with passion, love and exuberation, obvious our life is not in alignment with our purpose and aim. All human beings do not have the same purpose. Moreover the purpose may differ from time to time. After one objective has been achieved, we want to move, to another and a better ambition. It is a perpetual question, to which we have to go on seeking answers.

This is the route, which most people would like to take. But remember, in the last case, even the little effort is focussed. It is open to us, to decide , the most effective way, by using the 80/20 rule. But whatever route you follow, do not put upon yourself mental restrictions and barriers, that you cannot succeed, despite your best efforts. There is no definite formula for discovering as to what route is the most effective and suits you best. You have to discover it by trial and errors and by learning from your mistakes. ■■■

3

How To Be Always On Top and Being Cheerful?

A sure way of not being on the top, and always unhappy is to keep, everyone else happy. There is nothing wrong, in helping others. But, if you are doing it, at the cost of your own priorities, commitments and needs, you would always feel unhappy. You would invariably be feeling miserable on account of the fact that you have not been able to attain your cherished desires, goals and aims.

But at the same time, you must be aware of your own specific goals, in clear quantified terms. Your level of commitment, coupled with enthusiasm, and motivation, must match your goals. You have to, play big, for big goals. Your compelling reasons, have the power ,to over ride, any obstacle, which might be coming in your way.

Turn away from Losers

Another way, to be on the top is, to shun the losers and negative people, as they begin with the promises as to why something cannot be done and why you cannot attain your objectives. Avoid totally, the losers club, as it is impossible to change some of them. If you stick to them, you are bound to catch up and be infected by their negativity.

Keep on learning

You have to keep on upgrading and learning. This is the only way to improve yourself. There is no end, to the knowledge, you can gain. If you believe that you are a know all and do not need, to learn anything more, then bear in mind, that you have written the epitaph of your career. If you want to be successful, you need to spend sometimes on doing things in a better way. You have to keep on learning and learning more and more, so that you can go from one success to another. A basic characteristic is honesty and you must be frank, in admitting that what you do not know, you do not know.

Keep your Motivation Level High

You need to strive to keep your motivation level high so that, your compelling reasons for success, goad you, from one goal to another goal. They are aware that the road to success is rather rocky. Despite the obstacles and handicaps, you should not give up your journey half way.

Be Smiling

You are, under no obligation to accept as advice, something, which appears to be patently wrong and does not agree with your logic and reasoning. The idea of any activity should be to get happiness out of it. It is possible only, if you are clear, in your communication. Make it a point not to panic under any circumstances. A smiling face, will always, attract and impress people. You should be serious, as seriousness is, generally forbidding and gives wrong impression. You should never, try to be, what you are not. If you do so, chances are, that you would make a fool of yourself. A good posture and being yourself, gives a first-rate impression. We must bear in mind, that we cannot, all be perfect all the time.

Be unperturbed and Make others Comfortable

Not only you must be unruffled , and unflustered, but make all others also, who come in contact with you, comfortable. We should always try to live the life, we have dreamed of, not only tomorrow, but from right now. You must dream big to grow big. If there is one thing that separates the people, who are failure and people who are always on the top, is their tenacity. A basic thing, for being on the top and cheerful, is not only to strive, but attain financial independence. Life has various facets, like our family , professional and social life. We need to maintain a balance in all the areas of our lives, for our cheerfulness.

Live One Day At A Time

One way, to be happy, is not to carry, any kind of troubles, including what happened yesterday, or what you have now, or what you expect to have tomorrow. Quite often, the misfortunes we expect as the worst, never transpires. All worry or trouble, may not always be in mind. But remember that even that will pass away.

Don't give a lodging, to any kind of worry in your head. We can easily manage the burden of today. But it will be too much, if we added to it, what happened yesterday or what may happen tomorrow. Human nature is rather strange. We can dodge a lion, but not a fly or mosquito, which makes us fret. The best way to be on the top, is to live each day, as it comes and not to anticipate or dread the troubles of tomorrow, which may never befall . Do not torment yourself with the troubles, which have never arrived. Michel de Montaigne once said that *"My life has been full of terrible misfortunes most of which never happened".* ■■■

4

How to Manage and Resolve Conflicts in a Positive Way?

Conflict is normal. It is a part of life. It occurs, when there are differences between people, who can not agree, on their motivations, values, perceptions, or desires about events and other people . The differences may appear trivial on the surface. But in reality may lead to personal resentments.

It is a fact of life, that no two people, have the same approach to the same set of problems. By resolving the conflicts, we can maintain strong personal and professional relationships. All differences, need to be handled, in a respectful way, for the sake of keeping them, at a healthy level. You have to know , your actions and feelings and what has led to the conflicts, before you can resolve any differences and disputes. An important part, of sorting out, the differences of opinion, arguments, and quarrels, is to understand the cause, or causes at the back of disputes. It is equally applicable, to resolving the wrangles, between the nations and individuals, as well as in organisations.

The chief reason, for any conflict, is that some people, take a stand, that they are always right, and others must toes their line. Nobody is infallible, and the approach, that I am infallible, is the chief reason, for the conflict. Most reasons for conflict between the couples, families and organisations are petty. However, it is best, to resolve them, before the situation, goes out of the hand. Nevertheless, conflict resolution should not become a slanging match.

It is important to recognise, that any conflict resolution, should not be, at the cost of the your self-esteem or humiliation or accepting the demands of others, for buying peace. Basic truths and principles ,should not be sacrificed.

The idea, underlying the conflict resolution, is make pathways, creative problem solving, team building, and improved relationships. It is true that all of us, have different perceptions and needs. But the legitimate sources of conflict should be examined with an open heart.

While this approach, can be helpful, with people who are willing to concede, that the other could be occasionally right, it is a waste of time to argue with people, who have already made up their minds, that whatever they say, should be accepted as a gospel truth.

I am aware that all of us feel that our point of view is the best and unprejudiced. But I have learnt, with a long experience of dealing with matters, that quite often the gems of solutions, can come from the most unlikely quarters.

I have also realised that there is no finality to the methods of conflict resolutions. They need to be modified, improved or amended, as we move in life. You have to change your techniques, depending upon the persons and situations, you are dealing with.

For resolving conflicts, we need to be in control of emotions, so that we can convey our needs, without threatening , frightening and yelling. A conflict free atmosphere is conducive to a stress free life. For sorting out conflict, it is vital, to avoid, insulting, explosive, angry, hurtful and disrespectful language.

If it is indulged in, it puts the other party on the defensive and is guaranteed not to produce any worthwhile outcome. My approach in life is to avoid conflict, so that I can spend that much time on the things, which I cherish. I have deliberately developed a short memory, in the sense, that I try to forget any injury being done to me. I do not mull on any bad happenings again and again, to avoid filling my mind with hatred and dislikes against anybody.

I realise that my emotions in any given situation matter most to me and I am sure that this is equally applicable to the party, with whom it is proposed to resolve conflict. I like to go more than half way, to resolve any differences. I look upon my emotions subjectively and do not mix them with anger sadness and fear. I also realise that for emotional conflict resolution, strict logic and reasoning may have to be compromised.

As a District Police Chief, I found the police force under me, totally ignorant of the laws and the Mysore Police Act, as Karnataka was called in the 1960's. Logic and reasoning required that the police officials be sent for training and retraining to the State Police Training Institute. But I was told that there was a waiting period of 10 years to train the constables who were untrained. So I had my own training programmes organised with the resources at my command.

More than once, I had to sacrifice logic to solve a problem and to get good results. I had to overlook the defaults of the good workers, which should not have been logically done, in the interest of bigger and better interests. I have discovered that in resolving conflicts, non verbal skills like a smile, tone of voice, listening to others carefully, facial expressions, humour, laughter, postures, friendly gestures and a firm handshake are very useful.

Building trust is absolutely vital in crack conflicts. The idea is to reduce the size of conflicts and see things in a proper perspective. I believe, that for achieving anything worthwhile, we need to focus on our priorities, rather than, try to win any arguments or score any point. I also believe that everything including the conflicts will pass away.

Try to look in your life and recall, as to how many problems and conflicts of last year, you remember. With the passage of time, they look trivial and inconsequential. We should look to the future, and change the strategy and approach, of passing blames to others. Conflicts can be draining and they should be avoided as far as we can.

If you really do not want to surrender your space, make sure that you pick up your battles wisely. For resolving conflicts, it is vital to be willing to forgive and adopt a policy of give and take. Extend the courtesy of listening, to the reasons, for the other person being upset, so that you can understand his point of view. Also we should be willing to let go. It takes two people to keep a conflict going. If you can reach no agreement, then at least smilingly agree to disagree. ■■■

5

How to Make a Great First Impression?

Whatever, we may say, about some people with a golden heart or their being well meaning, the fact remains, that we form our opinion and judge people, the first time, we meet, or talk, or listen to them personally, or when we speak on phone.

We also form opinions even about the people we have never met, form some opinion, based on other factors. The other features, of our judging others, or others judging us, are based on, How we dress or walk, or converse.

Whatever you may feel, you cannot help, in not making the first impression. Even the impressions about the organisations are based, on the size, equipment, staff and building of its office, as well as how the receptionists handle the visitors or provide information.

A first time, good impression, is vital to our growth, progress and development. There are many occasions and ways, to make an excellent first impression. It could come in one to one meeting or while speaking on phone or in a small or a big business meeting. Our efforts should be to make a great first impression. It, of course, involves preparation and labour.

When we converse with others, we must make sure that our greeting, whether in person, or on our answering machine is friendly and professional. When you answer the phone and somebody asks you some information and you do not have it readily available, then note down what he or she wants. Tell the caller that you would get back and keep up your promise. Have a pad of paper and a pen, or a pencil handy, to take notes, near your phone. Before you make a phone call, jot down, what you want to say to others. Be an active listener. If you are in doubt about anything either about the caller's or other details, do not hesitate to ask for the same, rather than second guessing.

A good way of creating a good impression is to return all the calls made to you, promptly. The same could be, either, on your answering machine, or missed calls, on your mobile phone. This approach gives an impression of efficiency, enthusiasm, speed and promptness. But you must organize your thoughts before you make any call. It is vital to be concise but thorough with your facts before you place any call.

I like to make a short list of important items I want to discuss during the telephone call. If you are cheerful and smiling while speaking on phone, your enthusiasm, will get conveyed, as you cannot be smiling and grouchy, at the same time. Several studies have shown, that about 80% of the opinions, people form about us, from the response and tone of our voice. Only 20 % is the weightage carried by the actual words we use. A vast majority of people can assess our personality and mannerisms, through the tone of our voice.

If you have staff working for you, it is equally vital to check, once in a while, by making a call, by pretending to be strangers, as to how they react and respond to people calling your office.

When you are calling somebody, it is worthwhile, to ask, whether it is a good time to speak to him or whether he is free to talk or you should call, later on. It is because you might have called a person, when he might be busy with some meeting or talking on the other phone. He will always appreciate your consideration and thoughtfulness.

The idea of all these exercises, is to create a good impression and create a good image about ourselves, in the mind of the person we are meeting. Shakespeare said that "the whole world is a stage and we are all actors". We have to play a different role with our parents, our spouses and our children, colleagues, bosses and the people with whom we have personal and official dealings.

It is always best, to appear to be a friend to anybody we meet. Friendliness begets friendliness. A friendly and a sympathetic approach gets reflected in our body language. Body language is another form of communication, mostly comprehended by all of us. The idea is to start positive vibes.

When you meet people, meet smilingly and look straight into their eyes. If you are conversing in a sitting position, do not slouch and do not cross your legs or arms. If you are talking, stand straight.

A good posture adds and improves the impression, we make on others. Try to make an unconscious but positive emotional connection, with all, you meet. Never start any interaction with a complaint, as otherwise, you will start, with the negative tag of a complainer .

While it is in order, depending upon the receptivity, to add a tinge of humour, guard yourself against being sarcastic, as sarcasm can back fire. Do not adopt the approach of confrontation and proving to others, that you are always right.

Give up the urge and need to be right. This move has never helped, anybody in creating good impression. It is not likely to help you. You must first establish your credibility and competence.

Appearances count. Make it rule to be always well dressed. It is true, that the standards and ways of dressing, keep changing. A torn up jeans or a trouser with holes or shorts with sandals, may be a hit, with some youngsters. They generally give shoddy looks and form. The way we are dressed up, speaks louder than the way, we speak.

Better to be a little over dressed than under dressed. It is vital to be dressed relevantly for the occasion. Instead of mumbling, speak and enunciate clearly and not in monotone. Be lively both in your voice and facial expression, when interacting or meeting others. ■■■

6

How to Deal With A difficult boss?

Bad bosses and supervisors are a part of everybody's life. Nobody gets, a uniforml,. a good or a bad boss. Bad bosses are found in every business and profession and they are a fact of life. I myself had, in my career of over three decades, different, indifferent, difficult, testing and reasonable bosses.

Some of them were very decent, while others were pushy, or rude and down right insulting, to the point of being abusive. There was consistently not a fixed approach for dealing with each one of them. One had, to adopt different techniques, every time a new boss, came on the scene.

One thing, which was common, to all bosses, was their power, to make or mar one's career and further progress and promotion. To this extent, all bosses have complete control on the professional or personal lives of the people working under them. This is a powerful motivating factor, for the difficult bosses, to control their lives. People working under difficult bosses may be in position to correct the behaviour of the difficult bosses, but they must never lower their self esteem, by living in their constant fear. Unless one draws a bottom line, one's life can be in a mess.

The problem of a difficult boss, mostly arises, for the employees, when they get a new boss. A new boss has his own priorities and the ways of getting things done. Every person has a different approach.

But if people have been used to working in one particular way or ways, they find it upsetting, if asked to change, their work style or habits

I have been both a supervisor and supervised and have worked with at least different 50 bosses in my career.

I found that the best strategy, whenever a problem arose, was not to hesitate to consult my boss, as to what approach should be adopted. If it was not something suggested by the boss, which met my approval, I only politely put before him the alternatives available. At the end I would say, that Sir, I have given my view and the final decision is Yours.

I would also add, that whatever be his decision would be implemented with full sincerity and enthusiasm. This discussion enabled me to know the boss's likes and dislikes and also to understand his point of view.

It enabled me, to avoid any barbs even from the most harrowing bosses. After all, we must appreciate, that there can be more than one way to solve a problem and completing a task. I always believe, that I must not be dogmatic, that only my approach is right. There can be even better approaches, and methods of dealing with any problem. This manner has enabled me to tide even the most critical situations.

I have also made a rule, not react to verbal diatribe, or harsh criticism passionately. I have discovered, that verbal combats, not only with my boss, or bosses, but also with my colleagues and friends would get me into more trouble than I could anticipate.

If you react and enter into a feud, you increase the areas of conflict and differences. By keeping calm, you eliminate, any chance of falling to the bait of such a boss. Discussion rather than confrontation, should be your approach in dealing with a difficult boss.

Ask for the advice from the boss, the best approach to solve a given problem. It is better to prevent friction and conflict, than to make an effort, to resolve it, later on. Never look upon your boss as your friend, as both you and he are not equals in the organisation in which you are working. Friendships can be only between equals. Be professional in your approach to your boss.

Keep your personal life separate from the official life and never discuss, your personal matters with anybody in the office, which also includes your boss. Everybody had enough of his or her own problems and nobody wants to be burdened with the problems of others.Your approach should be to do your job well and carry out faithfully the instructions given by your boss, or as laid down by your organisation.

If you are criticised for poor performance, calmly introspect, examine and evaluate your own performance, whether you had done the assigned job appropriately.

It is better, to the extent, possible, to avoid going over the head of your immediate boss, to avoid rupturing of the relationship and criticism. This approach invariably breeds resentment.

However, if you have a toxic boss and feel that you are being targeted unnecessarily, then better document everything, and have a record of all such incidents, in your personal custody. Do not share it with anybody. This will be your main defence, if you are reported against by your boss. Also keep a record of what causes such a provocation.

At the same time, you should at the appropriate time, discuss your concerns with your boss. It should not be in any confrontational sense. Any discussion should be non adversarial and not, with a view to score points. Do not start your discussion with your boss, on the premises, as if you are the opposition party.

Courteous and diplomatic ways, of putting your concerns, with your boss, would rarely lead to any punishment or retribution. If you start with negative emotions, like counter attacking your boss, you will be engaging, in a self defeating behaviour, which will be, far from crafting, an atmosphere of problem resolving.

If you have been criticised justly, then look upon the criticism, as a valuable input to improve your performance and not as a personal attack. The idea of all such approaches is to have a stress free atmosphere. It also depends as to how you react, to a given situation. Some people may come under a great stress, in some circumstances, and while others, may not even feel a ripple.

List all the qualities of the boss which annoy you and rank them in the order of worst to less worst. Then prepare appropriate strategies to deflect or deal with them.

A study done in the USA, found that almost 80 per cent of the employees surveyed identified their boss as a lousy manager. Another study said that almost 70 per cent felt that their immediate superior had "no clue", as to, what to do, to become a good manager. One study estimated that 90 percent of the U.S. work force has been subjected to abusive behaviour at some time. The conclusions in the study were based on a survey of nearly 1,000 workers over eight years. The position in our country is not likely to be any different.

Lest this piece be misunderstood as a bad boss bashing, another survey found that 79 percent of workers respect their bosses a great deal. The employees rated the following traits in a good boss.

- Leading by examples
- Strong ethics or morals
- Knowledge of the business
- Fairness
- Overall intelligence and competence
- Recognition of employees

One thing, which must be, kept in view is that all of us, have a role of the boss, in some situations. Not all bosses are bad. One thing, that all of us can learn, is that, we should also try to be good bosses to the people we work with. There is no one size fits all solution, to all boss problems. We have to devise and invent a solution as we face problems and difficult people. ■■■

7

How to Understand the Body language?

We do not, communicate only, through our words, or the languages we use. Another equally important form of communication is the use of body language, or gestures, to convey as to how we feel about a given situation or how we react to others.

It is a non-verbal form of communication . For increasing our effectiveness, we need to use, the right body gestures, or movements along with the verbal language. In interviews for jobs, an experienced interviewer can judge the level of confidence, of the interviewee by the expressions, he or she conveys, by the body language.

Body language, can be both positive and negative. Quite often, our facial expressions, are sufficient to convey, our reactions or response. Nodding and the way you nod, can convey, your agreement or disagreements. Smiling or opening your eyes wider, showing enthusiasm and interest, is another form of body language. Body language can be, both apart or supplementary, to the verbal communications.

The negative response, is reflected in our frowns or by shaking our heads, or gritting our teeth or using any angry facial look, or an indifferent glance, or just turning our head or avoiding an eye to eye contact or using our index finger, to show our disapproval.

The design or intention, between positive and negative body language, generally shows, your response, in a way that corresponds, with the words you are using or are about to use.

There are plenty of gestures, you can use ,to learn and use your body language. When you can effectively use and learn, the use of body languages by others, it will enhance your effectiveness in life. By reading the body language of others, you can detect their moods or reactions or assess their personality without saying a word.

By acquiring the knowledge of body language, you can immediately discover, the view points and impressions, of others about you. You can become a human lie detector, by learning what the body language conveys.

It is rare and almost impossible, to be a perfect cheat or a liar. Either the body language, or verbal communication, would let out, the cat of the bag . By learning and recognising, what the body language conveys, you can decide about your strategy for dealing, with your loved ones, may be, your fiancée or a spouse, or your colleagues or your bosses.

By using this technique, you can make a dazzling, first impression, on the people, you meet, either for socialisation or for official dealings or for other work.

Quite often, the words are not enough, by themselves, to communicate, our competence, confidence and what we want . You need to combine them with the body language.

Using body language with the verbal communication, can definitely give you an edge over others. At the same time, both can be used, independently, if you so desire. Depending upon your skill, expertise and experience, you can use, the body language, to read people's mind and what they feel about you.

As a speaker, quite often, I look into the faces of the audience to decide, whether they are bored with my speech or I need to change the topic or change my line of reasoning or I should end my speech. In the first ten seconds, you can discover, by looking around carefully, whether, the other person is interested in you, or not, or whether, what you are saying is of interest to them.

Similarly when we meet people, we make judgement, based on their body language, about their nature , whether he or she is kind or tough, friendly or hostile, intelligent or otherwise. Every small actions of ours, gets communicated, by our gestures, to others, or of others, to us.

The most wonderful compliment, conveyed through words, will appear hollow, unless accompanied, by appropriate body gestures and language. Any mismatch, will dilute the effect or impression, we want to convey.

Learning body language can reveal and help, in easily identifying the liars, both in business and personal context. If you can interpret the signs, you can discover, whether the others, are being honest or deceitful with you, and whether they like you or not .

Our own body language signals, can also sway what other people may think or feel about us. If we do it rightly, we are likely to be liked and trusted. But even unintentional wrong signals, can affect us professionally, in our relationship, as well as career wise.

With a little practice and deeper observations , you can learn to be acquainted with the body language. Look at your closest friends or your nearest relatives or your well wishers. They will always be warm and affectionate, with good opinions about you. Compare their reactions, with the people hostile or indifferent or jealous of you.

Their body language, receptivity and interaction will be different. The motion of head, the smile and nodding are expressions of their body language. Turning face other side, or lowering heads, indicates, anything, other than liking or approving you.

A haughty head, and a severe look, shows that the other person may be itching for a confrontation with you. A lowering head shows, that the person has something to hide or he is ashamed of something.

Looking aside or away, can also reflect nervousness or trying to cover up lies, or feeling distracted. If somebody is, nice to you, at a social function, do not jump to the conclusion, that he is your friend or friendly to you. Do not mistake a few sentences, or drinks together, as a sign of love or attraction. Crossed arms, on the chest, or hands on the hips, only shows that such people might be tough to cultivate, as friends .

There are other body movements, like cleaning glasses again and again, or frowning, or raised eyebrows, or stamping feet or moving hands or feet while sitting which show restlessness, unresponsiveness and apathy.

Discerning body language is great way to discover the attitude of a person or his level of ggressiveness, boredom, pleasure and amusement. The eye contacts and eyes, reveal much more than any verbal communication. Learning body language, comes from observation and practice and is a great way to discover the feelings of others.

People may say one thing and mean another, but the body language is a great give away to the feelings and reactions of others. We all need to harmonize our body language to the occasion and the person, we are conversing with, in the interest of our maximum achievement. We should be constantly aware as to what our bodies and the bodies of others are saying.■■■

8

How To Deal With demanding and exhausting People?

All of us, have to interact with negative and difficult people, who might use the approach of hurting us, or at least, might have an intention behind their doing so. In every place, no matter where we go, we will meet people who are opposed to us or do not like us. With a billion plus people in our country, there is no corner, where you can avoid such people. Indeed conflict is a part of our existence,

We are no God, but the fact is that resentment and rancour, goes against us, much more, than against the person, who might be, the cause of it. We hurt ourselves, by being negative, as this way, we disturb our mental peace. When we fight back or react for any reason, it is just to satisfy our ego. It is essentially a battle between the two egos, that is of our own and that of the other person.

It is an unproductive battle, to show who is wrong or who is right. We waste our energy either in defending ourselves or in attacking others, for the sake, of our point of view. The same energy, can be spent in doing things, in a better way, for either ourselves or for the people we love, or for the well being of society.

Negativity in one area, leads to negativity in other areas. One reason, we feel hurt, is that, we do not like, what others say about us. Our Constitution guarantees freedom of speech, and we must accept that people are entitled to their own opinions, however, unpalatable it may be to us. As others have a right to express, their opinions, we have our own right to choose and select our response. It is upto each one of us to choose a response, of conciliation or peace or of fracas, or argument or of clash or quarrel.

I personally try to avoid any conflict or discord. This approach, makes for, a harmonious existence and a lot of mental peace. If you reflect deeply and cogitate, you would discover, that quite often, the cause of conflict either in the families or between friends or colleagues, would be something petty and not any earth shaking reason.

Instead of reacting instantly, it would be, worthwhile, to allow the tempers, to cool down. You would find yourself reacting differently, after you have considered the issue dispassionately. You may go even to the extent of questioning or asking yourself, whether it really matters, that you are right, if it is going to lead to a lot of unpleasantness and no gain to anybody.

It is best to avoid a negative response and to be dragged into negativity, even if others are trying to provoke you into it. By reacting, we are playing into the hands of negative people. This way, we snowball the cycle of negativity. We should make a conscious choice and a habit to stop draining our energy by thinking or acting negatively.

It is only fair to put ourselves into the other person's shoes to discover, as to why she or he has behaved or is behaving in a particular way. One which is obvious reason is that often such people behave in a way to force you to toe their line. If this happens repeatedly, it should not be taken as an aberration, but dealt with head on.

Instead of wasting time to improve the negative, unhappy and difficult people, cut out such people from your life. It is best to focus on your own happiness, rather than in wasting time, in reforming others.

Do not drain your energy and enfeeble your emotional strength, for any reason whatsoever.

Remember that you have no obligation, to your being, a universal reformer, at the cost of your commitment. Avoid all worked up and agitated discussions. This is to avoid feeling sorry, for having taken a particular decision or for saying something, which should have been better left unsaid.

If things go wrong, you do not have to go with them. Your efforts should be to drag away your beliefs and feelings from your pains and annoyances. Our troubles are exactly like difficult people, who become bigger and magnified, if you nurse and pander them.

Remember that difficult people and things are like devils, who are never the same when you confront them. Do not wring your hands, but roll up your sleeves, when you meet them, face to face. Do not treat every situation, you meet daily as a matter of life and death. We will meet all kinds of difficult people and face hardships in our lives, like the birds flying over our head. But it is upto each one of us to ensure that we do not allow them to build nests over our head. ■■■

9

How to Understand the Thin Dividing Line Between Success And Failure?

Nobody really wants to fail in life . Right from the humblest, in the huts, to the highest, in mansions, want success in the field, in which they are engaged. How is it that despite a fervent desire, only a small percentage, make it to the top.

One reason is, that if somebody fails once, in any venture, he takes the same, as final. What needs, to be borne in mind, that no failure, like any other situation, in life, is final and permanent. People who fail in life, trot many excuses, like that, they did not have the time. But the truth is that both the successful and unsuccessful have the same twenty four hours in a day.

By using the time, on the things which matter, the successful people have achieved enviable heights. By squandering the same, the failures have aggravated their conditions. It must be kept, in mind that success also means, from learning from the measures, as to why we, did not succeed earlier and why we have succeeded now. Success also involves pursuing your goal single-mindedly, without losing your zeal.

When you fail, ask yourself as to how many times, you tried and how many times, you refused to be cowed down by it. This is, only to assess, the level of your persistence. It is a bitter truth that success is linked to our persistence. We can do anything in life, as long as we stick to it, long enough.

It is a reality that failure is both demotivating and demoralising. But it is a fact of life that rarely any thundering success comes in the first attempt. The glory lies in falling down and getting up and trying again and again till you succeed.

If you are doing your best, and are busy, you will not have, any time to worry. The thin line between success and failure is illustrated by the fact, that most people desirous of success, do not try to find out the imperfection and then try to overcome them.

When Edison was asked about failure in inventing newer and newer things, before he invented gramophone and bulb, he replied that "I know now 10000 ways that won't work".

Our failure mostly lies, in no longer trying and giving up at the first obstacle. It is also a question, as to what you call failure. In my definition of failure, it is simply something, in which you have not succeeded yet. Never confuse one or two defeats, with the ultimate and final defeat. Treat failure, as an opportunity, to gird up your loins, and begin again shrewdly .

You can say, that you have failed half a dozen times, but never even remotely, auto suggest, to yourself, that you are a failure. You are not a failure unless, you have lost your courage to try again and again. No body succeeds through success. People succeed only through failures.

Failure gives us an opportunity to cogitate and discover as to what failures have led to our mistake. Mastering the mistakes gives us a chance to learn. It is only, through learning, that we can, acquire better skills, expand knowledge and enhance our abilities. It is only our skills and greater competence, which can make a difference to our lives and world. Better opportunities, come to us, only through our capabilities and expertise.

It is only through blunders and slip ups and by learning from them, that the most successful people have reached the top of their professions.

Slips up and errors, reveal to us, what would not work. Nobody starts, as a success from the beginning and day one. People have become great through experiences and mistakes. The important thing is not to stop and end your quest at the point you have failed.

If you give up at the first obstacle, and never try again, then it is curtains for you. Bear in mind, that what matters, is, where you end. Success does not come on easier terms, except by learning from your mistakes and then moving on. Never underestimate the power of your belief in yourself.

Do not lean, on others, to boost your confidence and build up your morale. Only you can do it, for yourself, by building yourself and trying again and again. Treat failure as a first step towards success. Even if you do not succeed, treat it, or, at the best, a deferred success. Any failure is not the end of the world.

Even a failure, in an examination, is not the end of the world. You can appear again, next time or next year. But you have to work more diligently and industriously to avoid failure. We should look, the fear of failure, in the face. It is only this way, you can gain courage, strength and confidence. Of course, experience, and especially failures is a tough teacher, as it gives the test first and lessons afterwards. Things, including our failure happen due to a cause and that cause lies within us. Cause could be your inadequate planning, preparations, failure to assess the right technique to deal with a problem. It lies within the capabilities of each one of us, to learn from our failure.

Nobody likes failure. If failure comes, despite your best efforts, then try to gain wisdom and lesson, from the same, so that you do not make the same mistakes again. Do not waste your life and time on regrets. Learn from what happened and why and then move on.

We must be open to change and be willing to adopt a different and newer strategy. But experience can teach, only those, who are willing to learn. Though man, has a unique quality of capability of learning from the mistakes of others. But at the same time, most men are disinclined to do so. So they make their own mistakes and then try to move on the right path.

No setback should be treated as tragedy and an unmitigated disaster. Instead, let us treat it, as a stepping stone to success. We should bear in our minds, the lessons of childhood.

A baby does not get up from the bed on birth and starts walking. It happens after one year. He or she often falls flat on his or her face, innumerable times, then pulls up and stands up, falls again and again tries.

Unfortunately, as adults, we forget the lessons of childhood. We tend, to treat our failures, or falls as permanent setbacks, rather than the essential steps in the journey to our final destination of success.

It is simply a question and will of crossing a thin line between our objectives from failure to success. In fact, you would not relish success, unless, you have tried your best. We must bear in our minds all the time, that success will not lower its standards for us. We have to come upto it. It is futile to divert your attention to imaginary troubles and worries, which may never come. Let us keep all the time, our own purpose, in our view irrespective of the circumstances we confront. ■■■

10

How To Find Purpose In Your Life?

Life presents us many chances and many opportunities. But what for, to use and encash them is both a challenging question and task. In other words, we need to find a purpose in our lives. The plain truth is, that quite often, a large majority of people do not have one. Or they are not able to discover the same. The main purpose, to put it plainly is the reason for our living and working. It is upto each one of us, to find a purpose, so that our life could centre around it.

Our purpose, if rightly discovered or revealed, should become our passion. The way to find purpose, is to list the things, you want to do and what comes naturally to you. In my own case, I like to read and write as through this way, I can gather all the knowledge that is available in the world. Similarly, each one of us can decide about the things, we should be wanting to do, without feeling or treating them as encumbrances.

A caution, which we need, to be borne in mind is, that, what we decide, should be our own purpose. It should not be somebody else's purpose and not something suggested by others . A purpose in life, gives a meaning to what and everything we do. It makes everything significant. It also guides and shows us, the way or direction, in which our life should be moving. It helps us in making big and small decisions in our lives. If you have more than one option, to do anything, it makes easier to decide, what to do and what not to do.

A purpose in our life gives us a foundation and base for leading a focused, decisive and rewarding life. Finding your life's purpose, is purely personal. There is no, one size fits all, or a universal formula for identifying and attaining it. Everyone, whether in the same organisation or in the family have their own different purposes. Even the twin brothers have a different and varied purposes as the goals in their lives.

There is no magic wand, which can give us instant results in finding purpose in our lives. Broadly, your purpose in life ,is strongly linked to what you are good at and what you do best, with your strengths.

A person strong in studies, would most likely be good in academics or research. A person who has a good voice, can try his or her luck in the field of music. A person, who is good, passionate and inquisitive, about science, has a better chance, in his avocation as a scientist. Find out what matters, to you most, and what improves the things, that are on your highest priority list, and you will most likely discover the purpose of your life.

Finding the purpose itself is not enough, unless you pursue it whole heartedly. Your life's purpose should fit your mission and statement of life. In any case, both are closely interlinked with each other. Their sole objective is, to bring about the kind of life, you want to lead and the profession, you wish to adopt and excel. Going after your definite aim in life is motivating. You can never succeed in achieving your purpose, if you hate doing what you are doing.

Says Christian D. Larson

"When you work simply for yourself
or for your own personal gain
your mind will seldom rise above
the limitations of the undeveloped personal life;
but when you are inspired by some great purpose,
some extraordinary project, all your thoughts
break bounds; your mind transcends limitations;
your consciousness expands in every direction;
and you find yourself in a new world, a great
world, a wonderful world; dormant powers,
faculties and talents become alive,
and you discover yourself to be a larger man by far
than you ever dreamed yourself to be."

You owe it to yourself, to discover your purpose. Then, if you reconcile it, with your profession and career, you will bring to it, unparalleled energy, ardour and passion. It will bring about a thunderous success, undreamt of, by you. Dream big dreams and you would realise them. It depends upon us, as to what we make of our life. Do not allow others, to choose the way, you should live your life. Living your purpose, enhances your self-esteem. Do not worry, about others may think of you, as long as, you are doing the right things and not harming anybody in the quest of your purpose in life.

Life is too short, to be spent, in being miserable and unhappy, which is the result of not having any purpose in life. We should seize life's moments to forge ahead in life in our chosen sphere of work. This is possible only, if we live our purpose, with a smile, feel confident and unstoppable. This in turn, will lead to overcoming all our fears, doubts, frustrations, anger, stress, anxiety, depression, bad habits or addictions.

Whining or moaning, about the things, we do not have, in life, is no substitute, for working hard and living our purpose. It would be better to spend that much of energy , in enjoying and getting things done, instead of lamenting. Life purpose, also involves getting out of our comfort zone. One thing must be clear that whatever we do, we are bound to meet disappointment, letdowns, catastrophes and challenges. They are an inseparable parts of life. We are bound to get more out of our lives, if we keep on trying and spend all the time in living our purpose.

■■■

11

How to Overcome Fear?

Fear thwarts us, in whatever task, we want to succeed. We all have, fears of either bullies, or snakes, poisonous insects, or creatures, like spiders, snakes or even darkness or of other kinds, like failure in examination or in achieving our goals.

Some fears are caused by our imagination, while some others can be real. The real fears, can be detected, by the acid test, whether it is something, which can damage, or hurt us, physically, financially or emotionally. If your fear is really dangerous, like the fear of burglars or dacoits, in case, you have a lot of cash, either on your person, or at home, then you will have to take preventive steps to avoid its recurrence.

If you are sick or afraid of any health problem, then it is wise, to consult an expert , or a doctor, in the field of his or her specialisation for guidance. Unless you confront your fear directly, and take action to meet it headlong, you would remain, in the same position, in which you are, at the time, you felt afraid.

To overcome your fears, you have to change the way, you think and change the way, you act. All of us, can think of one thing at a time, consciously. We should make, a deliberate effort, to put right and affirmative thoughts, of accomplishment and achievement in our minds.

Whenever any thought , which has a tendency, to drag you down enters your mind, you should make a deliberate effort, to stop it, in its tracks. Instead of feeling afraid and apprehensive, think of the opposite. In other words, you have to defend yourself, against dreadful and awful thoughts, by confronting them with the admirable and first-rate beliefs and feelings.

You have to intentionally, methodically and consciously, programme yourself with the positive convictions every day. Your efforts should be to replace, fear thoughts, with the fulfilment thoughts. What we generally imagine, is by and large far, from the truth. Quite often, it is not even near it.

None of us is born with either courage or fear. Our fears are brought about, by our own beliefs or exposure to some unpleasant situation or predictions caused by others, or superstitious columns in some print media or TV Programmes.

Some fear, like walking alone in the night or at odd times in crime prone areas are valid. It is a common sense, to avoid such timings, areas and situations. We can finish off our fears, by taking preventive action. Once we circumvent, evade and decimate our fears, we can lead a high quality life. Bear in mind, that even an elementary fear, can destroy our enterprise and ambition. It is one of our biggest enemies, apart from indifference, indecision, worry and doubts.

We all have limits. Though each one of us is something, none of us, is everything. It is true, that we might be deceived, and let down, if we trust too much. It is also a fact that if we do not trust enough and delegate enough, we may not do or get done, all what we want to have done. This way, we will be tormenting ourselves too much.

You have to take a chance on it. Our fear steals our chances of a better future, as it leads to our drifting in life. If we are fearful, we do not encash, on the opportunities, which might come our way.

I myself have postponed many decisions, due to my scepticism. I used to ruminate on the events and time gone, and on what is going to happen in future. I recognized, that it did not pay at all to be scared, anxious, and apprehensive about the things which have not happened, and which may not happen at all.

I have also appreciated that it is futile to regret over the past, which is dead, gone and over. What matters is present and so I make it point to focus on it, to make it fear free.

What matters most often is boldness and not timidness. To overcome fear, we have to constantly battle with it and build up our strength for attaining our goals and aims.

Courage is, what is required at all the time, to build up our strength and to overcome fear. If you are a religious type, then, as many religions preach, you can take all your fears and concerns to God and ask Him to handle the same. The only way, you can become stronger is to face your fear, by a Natural , but unseen Superpower.

When you face your fears boldly, you will find the fear slinking away. It is exactly like calling a bully's bluff, who will shrink away, on being challenged.

From a distance and in our mind ,things may seem very complicated, thorny, and hard, but when you actually have a go at them , you will find them, surprisingly easy. What is important is to take action as inaction produces doubts and fears. It is only through action that you can generate confidence and courage. Be bold to overcome your fears and you would find mighty forces coming to your aid, unseen , and unheard. ■■■

12

How To Get Rid of Ego?

Ego is variously known as self-esteem, self-image, or an opinion, of one self, or our self worth. There is a line of difference between the ego and pride or a sense of superiority. An egoistic person believes, that what he says is not only valid but is eternally true. He does not accept any merit, in the opposite point of view. The fact is, that there can be, truthfulness and accuracy in other person's point of view.

Truth is not a matter or an issue, of right versus wrong. Truth is essentially the honest facts, reality and uprightness. The fact is, that an egoistic person, seeks to impose a command or a control on others. It might not be, done directly. It can be done subtly.

An egoistic person is not only self opinionated, but also seeks to impose his proposals or designs on others. He or she is averse to suggestions from other. It is vital, to bear in mind, that every point of view has some element of truth in it. We need to recognise it, to overcome our ego. A self-centred person, would raise objection to everything and to every point of view, except his or her own.

Every point of view has some element of honesty and reliability. While we may not agree with it, we must try to be open minded, that there can be different points of views on any subject.

When we are logical, lucid and judicial, we come out of our egoistic thinking, or positions. When we are rational and have a sagacious approach, and may realise that our stand is indefensible. It has happened to me more than once, when I have given up my stand and accepted other's point of view.

We must realise that none of us is the repository of all intelligence and wisdom in the world. Sometimes and more often, than not, we are averse to finding holes in our reasoning and thinking. What comes in between, us and the right decision, quite often is our ego.

The important thing, is to recognise the truth in the points of view of others, however, unpalatable it may be to us. We must recognise and accept that people are made differently and have different upbringing, and professional competences.

Nobody is a copy of any body. It is not possible to stream roll everybody, to one particular type. Ego can kill our core skills. We need a constant awareness, to correct ourselves. It not easy to do, as it requires synchronisation, between our thoughts and action.

You have to check yourself, often to correct yourself, whether you are feeling superior in a given situation or whether you are angry, because our ego is getting hurt, over somebody's actions.

Of course, it must always be borne in mind that there is a very slender demarcation between our ego and our pride. We have to guard ourselves, about the transformation of our ego to our pride. An easy and straightforward way of discovering and perceiving it, is to assess yourself, whether you are considering, others inferior to you.

Some of us, may have higher station of life, but the reality is, that as human beings, we are all equal. In India, there is a tradition of people touching the feet of the elders or seniors. I have never allowed anybody , including children and adults to touch my feet. I tell them, that we are all equal as human beings. When we act from our ego, there is envy, strife, anger, contention, resentment, selfishness, jealousy, and avarice.

We keep these emotions alive, by feeding them with our thoughts. It is in our own personal interest, health and emotion to keep our ego at bay.

Whenever our parents or our bosses feel unhappy or express disapproval about our performance, or any other work, we feel very gloomy, miserable and demoralised. It has happened to all of us at one stage or the other, of our lives. The answer to this is, to see the things, from the other's point of view. Doing the best, may not be good enough for the others, who may have different standards to judge us, what we have set.

In any case, it is in our own interests to get rid of our ego, as it will mean cutting out anger, hatred, disgust, dislikes and resentments, out of our lives. Bear in mind, that we do not like, ego in others and feel that such people are unnecessarily throwing their weight about. Surely, nobody, like wise, would approve of ego in ourselves. If we do not like some qualities in the rest of mankind, we should take into consideration and apply the same standard to ourselves. Our ego is our greatest self sabotager. It is definitely, not our real self. Our ego wants to see things, either as black or white or as right or wrong. While there is nothing wrong in being self-confident or proud of one's achievement, there is everything wrong in being egoistic and in taking everything which happens to us, personally. Ego breaks the bonds between friends, because of self-centredness of the egoist and spoils relationships. It is a plague, which is got rid off sooner, than later. ■■■

13

How To Deal with Difficult People?

We are all different people and everybody is a difficult person, for somebody else, at sometime, or the other. Keep in view that people are not behaviours. They behave or what some may call misbehave, when they feel threatened or cannot get their way, or when they meet unpalatable circumstances. People can change as their circumstances change. People are vital living human beings with a wide range of spectrum.

In spite of all what we may perceive, there are certain people, in our lives, whom we cannot stand, because of their behaviour, of either being of aggressive or passive propensities and dispositions. All human beings have a pattern of behaviour. Quite often we can anticipate the same and so we prepare ourselves suitably, to react, to them. Human beinns are endowed with different qualities, in the sense that some are always Yes or No Men, or May be or Whining or Know All, or people, who would always be acting, as bullies or complaining or being please all.

The conflicts arise, when the qualities, or inclinations of individuals, do not match. There are some people, who would like, to get the things done right. There are others, who make themselves difficult, in their craving for appreciations or recognition and when they fail to get the same, either deservedly or undeservedly, they become difficult.

It is a fact, that degree of knowledge , education skills, approach, and the ability to communicate, varies from individual to individual. Aggressive, passive, bragging, emotional, and negative people can be difficult to deal with, as diverse methods and course of action are required, to deal with each category.

While negative and aggressive people, may make you, feel thwarted, or passive, the yes men, may frustrate you, for lack of any contribution to your life or work. At the same time, bear in mind that you may be annoying and trying several people around you. This is due to the fact, that each one of us, is a difficult person, at some time or the other, for others. It is best to end the negative relationships, which cause discord, tension and friction. The less clashes, conflicts and collisions, you have in life, the more efficient and more happier, you would be.

I myself have noticed, that any wrangle, however justified it may appear to me, leaves me unhappy. A contact or a relationship, which is supportive, is conducive, to peace and harmony. If the conflict is with a person, with whom contact is unavoidable, as he is a member of the family, or the boss, then the best course, is to avoid discussing contentious issues, which can lead to arguments and differences of opinion.

Even otherwise, it is best to avoid issues, like religion or role of politicians or personal appearances, or any other subject, which can augment bitterness.

If others try to involve you in such a situation, where there can be arguments, you can always get out of the situation, by saying that everybody has his own opinion and view point, without expressing your own.

Whenever, some body has tried to drag me, into a contentious issues, I just keep quite or say, for the purpose of deflecting argument, that I am not an expert in the matter.

I have also observed that it is futile to change any difficult persons, through your wisdom and intellect. Whenever I had tried to do so, it led to criticism and made things, more difficult.

Whatever be the position or situation, never accept or tolerate, abusive, insulting or a rude behaviour, from difficult persons. Otherwise, the difficult person would think, that he has bullied you.

You are, under no obligation, to accept any snub, rebuff, affront or slight from such a person. It is upto, you to avoid any contact with such a person, unless, you are officially or personally placed in a way, in which you cannot do it. Still you must have clearly demarcated boundaries, beyond which, you should not allow the difficult person to cross.

You do not have to go out of your way to please a difficult person. If you need any support, do not look upto any difficult person, who might have made your life harsh and demanding. Do not share your personal life or your secrets, with a self-centred, and a trying person, who might have already made life tricky, problematic, and callous for you.

Get the fulfilment of your needs from others, who are supportive of you, rather than from the difficult person. If you are going for a walk and you are likely to run into your tormentor, or a difficult person, then change your route, to avoid any sarcastic confrontation, or remarks.

Know when to distance and cold shoulder, yourself, from difficult people and then do so. You should let go relationships with such people and cultivate people, with whom you can co exist harmoniously and positively. You do not have to blame yourself, for the conduct and negativity of the difficult person. Be polite to all including the difficult person, but never try to develop intimacy with them. Never give your confidence to him, if you want to lead a happy life.

■■■

14

How To Make The Most of Your Mistakes?

When we say something, which offends others, and we realise, that it is a mistake, it is best to offer regrets. This is one way, to keep the stress at bay. Not offering apologies, when it is called for, can be stressful.

We should learn from our mistakes. This is one way, to be responsible for our life and work and move on. The real problem is our ego, which comes in between, us and the admission of our mistakes. Living with a belief, that one is infallible, and will not make a mistake, is to live under an illusion.

It is also passing up the opportunity, to learn from our mistakes, instead, of later on, berating ourselves, over them. Constant evaluation of our mistakes and possible wrong steps, is the only way to learn, as well as avoid them, in the future.

List the situations of which you are afraid of and imagine the worst that can happen. Imagine you are being bullied by some body. What is the worst that can happen, if you stand up ? Either the bully will back down or you would have a confrontation with him.

There are little chances of any bully aggravating the situation, because the bullies are generally used to having their ways. Or if you ask, for a raise in your job, have no apprehension, that you would be sacked, though you may be afraid, that it might happen. If you do not reveal your intentions, as to, what you expect from others, how will they know it.

It is more painful, to have fear of something, than not acting and feeling frustrated daily. You have to burn bridges behind you and take action. The only way to overcome any fear is to spot it. Face it headlong rather than spend any energy in avoiding it.

You can overcome any fear by repeatedly doing precisely, the thing, which makes you fearful. Most of us, from childhood have been exposed to the idea, that asking for help or assistance is not good and shows ourselves in a poor light.

This conditioning is generally carried on, to our adult lives. If you still feel doubtful, ask yourself, as to what purpose, you are making any request. If you go to the root of the problem, you would find the answers. Your asking for help should not be a one way traffic. When you are requested for help, or when you have an opportunity, you must return the favour , not only to those, who have done something for you, but also to others.

The ultimate aim of our life is to attain our goals and reach our targets. Our endeavour should be to win and not merely to try. We either succeed or do not succeed. There is nothing in between, whatever some people may say.

You should not say that you 'tried'. It only shows a defeatist attitude. If you start something, keep on it, till you have attained. You may not realise, as to what you may not get, by not trying. The idea is, to set your target and keep on trying, till you reach it.

It is a part of life to run into walls and obstacles. It will be fool hardy to go and bang into the walls, while trying to reach your goal. You must either go around or over it.

We should not be averse to taking help, though many people are reluctant to ask for it. We fail only when we quit. But only we can take this decision and nobody can do it for us.

You should not accept any excuse from yourself, as an alternative or a justification for not getting success. No miracle is going to get you out of any problem. You are the miracle, as well as a miracle maker. Whatever be your situation, always keep on, telling yourself, that you can do it.

No body can have perfect conditions at all the time, whether it is the family or health or relations. If you are, given a responsibility, to perform a particular work or complete a particular job, do not start, with a pre-conceived notion, that it is not going to work.

Do not look upon the responsibility entrusted to you as a burden. If you cannot be positive, all the time, the least, that you can do is to stop spreading negativity. Do not be judgemental by saying that "it won't work," unless you have given it. Even then any set back is temporary and there is nothing permanent about the failure. Remember that if you cannot contribute, do not come in the way of those, who would like to contribute. If you want to control your destiny and your future, you must, above all, shed negative attitude. Relate your action goals to your life goals. This is the only way, you can empower yourself. You must be passionately committed to your life goals, and if you are working for somebody else or an organisation, their goals should be your goals. This way, you can add value to yourself and make yourself indispensable. Of all the forces that make for a better world, none is so indispensable, none so powerful as hope. So long as you do not give hope, be sure that anything is possible. ■■■

15

How To Grab A Golden Opportunity?

There are many things, of which we are theoretically aware, but do not or half heartedly, implement them. For example, all of us are conscious of the fact, that when we cannot do our best or are feeling tired, then it is, rather over due, to take a break and rest. But still people keep on working with a magical belief or expectation, that they must complete their work.

Each one of us, has the best time, for doing our best work. If we can use our prime time, for our prime work, then the results can be outstanding. Rest is like a fuel to the body. It sharpens our senses and sensibilities, about whatever, we may want to accomplish. If you do not take rest, when you should be resting fully, then you would not be working, when you should be working, at your optimum levels.

If you are mentally tired, then you are, neither here nor there. While it is alright, to push yourselves, harder and harder, for achieving higher and higher attainment, we should not punish ourselves, without giving ourselves a breather and time for relaxing and unwinding. None of us, is under obligation, to neglect our own needs, for the sake of others.

At one time, I used to put more on my plate, than I could chew. It was, in the form of accepting, more and more engagements and commitments, and tiring myself out at the end of the day. It is no use, making yourself miserable to make others happy.

It suddenly dawned on me, that it was not only counterproductive, but also left me, in a condition, in which, I could never give my best. We should learn to spend time, on the things, which matter, most to us. We should not compromise on them, for the sake of pleasing others.

For relaxation, different people can have different approaches. I, personally like, to read a book of jokes, before going to sleep or some book, which cheers me up. I also avoid the company of all those people or things, which depress me.

You must all the time, feel good, if you really want, to get the best out of yourself or give the same to others. Only this way, you can write a glorious future, for yourself. We should not live life, as it comes and goes, without caring as to how we should be functioning or working.

It will be a good idea, to remind yourself in a note form, as to how you want things to turn out in the next one, two or three or five, or ten years time, in your life. From time to time, you should be able to compare your achievements against your goals and what dreams you have been able to attain. You can even write a letter to yourself, as to where you want to reach in life on a particular date or year.

This is just one way to determine, whether your career and life has gone as planned or whether you have exceeded your expectations or fallen short of the same. This approach can be a morale booster. If you want to achieve something in life not only, you should strive for the same, but also feel good, while taking action. If you are feeling, upset or frustrated, in taking any action, you cannot make any progress.

Feeling good, is the best way, to be in alignment with your goals. There is a price, or dues, to be paid for everything and the price includes, to have good thoughts and feelings.

A secret or rule for moving forward lies in doing, what we feel, motivates us to attain our goals. Our definition of feeling good is individual and specific. It need not be, what is laid down by experts or others known to us. You cannot reach 'heaven', by following a hellish path. To determine, what makes you feel good, is to follow, your own internal guidance and thinking. There is no better expert on you, than yourself.

Feeling good also includes eliminating from your life, what does not make you feel good. It could be anything, you do not want to do or eliminating obstacles coming in your way of feeling good. One good input, for feeling good or happy, is to force yourself, to be happy and to smile. Your target should be, not only to make you happy, but also to bring happiness and joy in the lives of others.

Get rid of the mental burden and obstacles, in the form of, what others think about you. It never feels good to worry about what others think of you. By worrying or by trying to get the approval of others, for anything or everything you do, you are adding a mental burden to yourself.

Be sure that there is no dearth of fault finders, who would never be satisfied, with anything or everything you do. It is not only your bosses who will tell you how to be better, but most people around us, function as unpaid universal advisers on every single issue under the sun.

It never feels good to worry about others and what others think of you, as long as you have done your job well. It is the biggest handicap to worry about what others think of you.It is not for us, to make others happy. Everybody and each one of is responsible for his or her happiness. No one is going to hand it over , to you on a platter. ■■■

16

How To Make Your, Wish List, A Reality?

There are certain things, we do in life, on automation. When we go for a walk or other exercise, or eat our food or take a walk, we take action without any serious thinking. We do not think, whether we should walk to the east or western direction, as long as, there is a clean place available.

It is for us, to make life, happen, on the lines we want it to be. You have to go on introspecting, to discover, whether you are achieving, to your full potential. If, despite your best efforts, you are still not achieving, the anticipated or expected results, it is a challenge for you, as to what and how much more you need to do.

The only requirement is, that you should be willing, to do, whatever it takes to win the game of life. However, most people feel, that despite their best efforts, they remain where they are. It is because they are not in a position or do not control the flow of their life. The most vital thing is, to take control of your life and do whatever matters most to you.

A friend of mine constantly complains, that he has no time, either for his family, or for doing the things he wants to do. I asked him, to write down for seven days as to how he spent each minute of his life on those days.. He was reluctant, but he did so. I further asked him, to analyse, as to what he did was in accordance with his desire and goals. He unwillingly came out, that he spent two hours on gossiping, three hours in sitting in front of a TV and another two hours on telephone. I further probed him, as to how much of it was helpful to him professionally. He admitted that only 5% of the time so spent, could, at the best, be called work related. Naturally, he was not getting the desired results.

You have to cut out of your life, the things, that do not or marginally matter to your goals and aims.

For changing your state of affairs and circumstances, you have to be in command of your life. You must be clear, as to how you should work and live your life. You cannot add to the 24 hours given, to each one of us. But you can. by being in charge of it, take control of it, decide as to on what matters, most to you. The most vital secret and weapon for success, is to regulate and have power over your life. This is not something to be done periodically, but for every minute of our life.

If things still do not go on, as planned, do not blame anybody, but check your own strategies and approach. Talk to the people in your profession and develop your own early warning system, so that you can take corrective steps, where you feel, that you are deviating, from your chosen path of encashing on openings and chances that might come your way.

Identify the resources, you can use, to apply to the achievement of your goals. Do not be apologetic, in asking for advice from others, so that you do not have, to invent the wheel. Write down all the difficulties, however small, that seem to recur in your march to your intended destination.

Collect all possible difficulties, which you are facing now, or might confront you in future. Theorise as to their possible cause and put them in writing in a note book. Then use the same, in generating innovative ideas and possible changes, in fixing the difficulties. Observe and scrutinise the best practices, which have made other people achievers and successful.

Dynamic innovation is the key to success. You have to determine your own hindrance, obstruction and snags. After doing so, you need to develop and discover your own issue solving style in your own assignment. This is the only way, by which you can uncover, what works best for you, in a given situation. You will probably locate several alternatives, and one of them will be greatest and most excellent for you, for dealing with a particular issue or a set of issues. Apart from meeting the knowledgeable people, another resource for dealing with the problems would be the library or internet. One caution, no one method is a permanent panacea for dealing with all the problems, difficulties, men and matters. You have to justify even to yourself, as to why you have made a particular decision. Remember, all change and all success has a price tag and you have to be willing to pay for it. You should examine the price to be paid, with reference to what you are paying now, for not reaching your destination. You have to pay a price for becoming the controller of your life and destiny. So far as I am concerned, I do not know much about luck and have never banked on it. Luck for me is hard work, and distinguishing between what is opportunity and what is not and then make the most of it. ■■■

17

How To Use A Magic Formula for Success?

Success in any venture, is dependent upon your knowledge, competence and dedication to achieving a given set of results. If something does not work, then we must get feedback, as to what caused its failure. Our achievement depends upon, the feedback we get and how we react to it.

The problem is, that we are generally rooted, in habits and ruts and so function accordingly. We need to change our practices, pattern, and approach to anything, and everything with the changing environment and milieu, if required. It will mean changing our thinking. While we want to change, yet we generally abhor taking risk.

It should be kept in mind that we may not succeed all the time, and we may not fail all the time. Precision, about what we want is the key to success.

We must be open to develop a flexibility of behavior. We must realise that every person is unique in his own way and the method of one may not necessarily suit others. We cannot control other people and their conduct, as well as other events, but we can change our response to them.

Before we can change others, we must be an example to others and keep on learning from everyday events. Things remain the same. Only we have to learn to change. We have a choice, as to what attitude, we adopt. Attitude is, after all, an established way to responding to men and matters.

Our attitude gets reflected in our behavior and conduct. Our reactions to others, which is also reflected in body language is our reaction to a particular person or an event. This way, without even speaking, we send out a message of our like or dislike to others. While generally have a choice of attitudes. Sometimes, the attitude of others compels us to take a particular course of action, inspite of our best efforts. If somebody is, out to assault you, then, either you can hit him back or be hurt by him or quietly go away, after being hit. So despite our best efforts to be nice and reasonable, we tend to adopt an attitude, which normally we would not.

Remember, that there is a time to be courageous and a time to be afraid. We finish ourselves and lives, the day, we become silent about the things that matter. However, it is upto each one of us, to learn every day from every event.

Nevertheless, it is vital to give our best to whatever we do. 75% success consist of showing up. If you enjoy your work, you are bound to be successful. Many geniuses, including Edison, have said that genius is 90% perspiration and only 10% intelligence and hard work.

Opportunities are galore. The only thing is to encash on them, by sharpening our skills. Whenever you face a verbal assault, attack, and are accused, your goal must be to command respect because sensible people do not attack people they respect. Antagonistic, vicious and destructive people require a powerful and vigorous responses. Your behaviour, towards them , must send a clear signal that you are strong and capable, since anything less than that, will invite further attacks. But you must do so, without coming down to his or her level.

Whenever you face an obstacle, come out with three solutions and keep on brain storming as to how best you can handle any given situation. Make a habit to be solution oriented rather than an alibi man. There are no quick fixes or magical solutions to the problems of life, except, that you have to continuously, go on devising newer and newer methods of dealing and overcoming them.

For being at the top of your efficiency, you need to confine yourself, to your own work and not interfere or become a universal adviser, as to how, others should work or behave.

Of course, if you are a boss, you need to review the work of your time, to the extent of making sure that they are on the right track and are performing, as required or expected. You must appreciate, that an intelligent person, does need to be told the same thing twice. Do not take responsibility, as to how to run other's life or business.

Instead of saying, that man is the creature of circumstance, it would be better, to hold fast, to the belief that man is the architect of circumstance. One way, to be successful is to make it, a point to do something every day that you do not want to do. This will help you in acquiring the habit of doing your duty to your job, profession and yourself without any pain.

There are a number of scapegoats, which most people use for their failure in not being to achieve their goals. The most accepted and popular, of the scapegoats is the God or Luck. Do not fall into this trap. Do what you have to do, with all your heart and competence. This is the only way to realise your ambitions. Remember that there is no commandment or advice or a precept, which does not have something inconvenient about them.

By our will, we can shape the future. Whether you fail or succeed, shall be, by your own doings and not of the others. It is for us to clear any obstacle before us, or be lost in the confusion and labyrinth. It is our choice; our responsibility; to win or lose. It is we, who hold the key to our destiny. The only alternative, before a wise man is to gird up his loin, give blood and sweat for his or her quest. ■■■

18

How To Develop Effective Communications in life?

Communication is basic to success in any undertaking or a venture. Unless, we can communicate, as to what we want, there is no way, we can get things accomplished to our satisfaction through others.

The problem is, that people are not able to say, as to what they want to say. If they can say something, it might not, necessarily, be the best way. The main reason, for poor communication is, that people do not pay full attention, to listening to others. The important thing, is to listen with heart and not with, preconceived notions, in our head. The result is, that in such situations, what we say, is based on our past unpleasant experiences with others. Sometimes, we anticipate without listening to what a particular person is going to say and react accordingly. The result is, that we place, our own interpretation, as to what anybody is going to say and respond so.

We must clearly understand, that our capabilities to communicate touch every area of our lives. Anything we do, in life, necessitates communication with others. Communication can be both oral and written. It is, through effective communications, that individuals or corporations, are able to achieve excellent results.

Without proper communications, we will not even know, whether we have come upto the expectations of our bosses or whether the people working under or with us, have performed upto the desired levels or are lagging behind in targets. Even in our personal lives, if we do not communicate properly and efficiently with our families, we are likely to jeopardise our relationships with our spouses or other family members.

Communication, in reality, is a two-way street and a process. It is a continuous activity, and not a one-time occurrence. The role of listening and a listener, or a speaker is vital to this process. Real rapport can be established only if the communicator and the communicated participate in it efficiently.

For purposeful communications, we also need, to develop our listening skills. If you are doubtful, whether your points and ideas have been clearly understood, there is no harm, in asking others, whether you were able to convey your messages clearly. Eye contact between the listener and speaker and suspending any evaluation or judgement, on anything which is being said, is a good habit to cultivate.

We all have, our personal likes and dislikes, of both persons and events. It is something, which cannot be wished away, as all of us are the products of our upbringing, culture, life experiences and what has been handed down to us by the society, our parents and our teachers. We should try, to put our personal triggers, in the background and listen to what others are saying.

If we have pre-conceived notions, then they considerably shut or reduce our listening attention span. List the behaviours and habits, you want or need, to change, to improve your listening quotients. The best thing is, to fully and completely listen to others and not to formulate your response, till that time. Make a conscious effort, to identify, what comes, in the way of listening, of your ability, to listen to others. This approach will enable you, to have a full picture in front of you, before fully communicating or reacting to any situation.

A study shows, that we have capabilities of thinking upto 500 words per minute. The speaking rate, can vary from 100 to 140 words a minute. As the speed of thinking is faster, than the speed of talking, or conversation, this can lead, to break up in communication or even an incomplete or a garbled communication. If you want to be effective, listen to everything that is being said respectfully and fully and then only respond. We should listen to what is being said and not presume, as to what is not being said. A golden rule in good communication is to listen twice as much as you speak.

Effective communication is one of the essential tools, we need in life. Nobody is born with it. We develop them in the course of lives.

Use simple language. Your objective should be to express, and not to impress. You should not hesitate to ask questions if you feel that some point is not clear to you. Try to handle people with a little tolerance, sympathy and kindness, while speaking. This will be a good preparation to communicate effectively. Real communication is not about glib talking, but talking to others successfully. ■■■

19

How To Succeed in Life?

There are various guidelines, for succeeding in our lives and professions. But no principle works, in the world, unless we do. One thing, I have noticed, is that when something needs doing, then it has to be done just and should be done.

My own experience shows, that if I put off, doing something, even temporarily, then it gets delayed. If further delayed, the delay gets multiplied. More than that, we tend to forget, or are overtaken, by other urgent or pressing tasks. I received a request from my publisher, sometimes back, to write the preface, for my next book, the manuscript of which, I had sent to him. He also asked me to suggest some names for the title of the book. Though I was feeling down cast, due to the death of a close relative, I just sat down, started working on it. Lo and behold! I had finished it in two hours, revised it again and emailed it.

It suddenly dawned on me, that the biggest secret of achievement was, to sit down and persevere to do whatever, I had to do. Perseverance and constancy of purpose, is the only virtue, by which, you can achieve a glorious success. Striving and achieving success, washes away the sweat and labour, in achieving it.

Success has various definitions and one given by Emerson, which is my favourite is as under;

"What is success? To laugh often and much; To win the respect of intelligent people and the affection of children; To earn the appreciation of honest critics and endure the betrayal of false friends; To appreciate beauty; To find the best in others; To leave the world a bit better, whether by a healthy child, a garden patch or a redeemed social condition; To know even one life has breathed easier because you have lived; That is to have succeeded".

Others feel, that success is that old ABC- ability, breaks and courage. We have to pass failure, on the way to success. You cannot change life, as it happens to you. But you can make a success of it. You have to unconditionally accept and make the best of it. Everything bows down to success.

If for some reason, you do not succeed, do not speak ill of the people around you, as well as of the world, in revenge, as some people do. It will make you miserable and at the same time, not solve any problems. Just saying, that you are doing your best, is not enough. You have got to succeed, in doing what you have set out to attain. The toughest thing, about success is , that you have to, go on succeeding to maintain your reputation. You cannot succeed without hard work, just as you cannot harvest where you do not plant.

If you try, to please everybody, in everything you do, or want to do, then you would be a sure failure. Success is not, a one day affair. You should be ready for failure, at times, for months and sometimes for years, before you can succeed. Form a habit of doing things, which must be done, instead of putting them off, for one reason, or the other.

Not liking, or willing to do things, which are a must, makes people a failure. You must become so professionally competent, so that, you become indispensable to your organisation. Give your job, the best you can, and at the same time, be prepared to seize the opportunities, which might come your way.

You not only have to master the job, but also yourself, without vacillating. It takes, as much courage and effort to have tried and failed, as it takes to have tried and succeeded. All success is based on courageous decisions.

Guts to climb up and take a chance are the prerequisite of all achievement. You may not be the smartest, or most talented person in the world, but you are bound to succeed, if you keep on going, going and going. The victory in our world ultimately belongs to the most persevering. Success is an ongoing exercise. If a businessman stops, all his activities, at a given point, that he is successful and need not do more, he is bound to be left behind, in this age of new technology and new inventions.

At one time, cordless telephones, where you could speak from any point in your house, was the ultimate in riches. Now is the age of mobile phone, which you can use from anywhere in the country, including in the moving vehicles and trains. Most businessmen in the business of telephones have changed to mobiles or other adopted other lines, for the simple reason that old landlines, though still existing have been replaced by the newest types of gadgets. Not only you have to hang on, for your success, after others have given up, you have to make sure that you continue doing so, till you succeed. This is the ultimate secret of success. ■■■

20

How To Get The Most Out of Life?

For success in our work, we need to be organised, disciplined, as well as have a capacity to take action, and communicate well. If we try to do everything ourselves, chances are that we may not either do it satisfactorily or make a mess of it. There are ways of either delegating to others, who know those jobs well, or preparing your check list, to make sure that no part of the work is neglected. Do not insist on doing everything yourself. You do not get recognition for doing everything yourself, but in attaining your goals. Check lists should be prepared not only when you are doing a task, but also to cross check, whether the delegates selected by you have covered all the points.

Having checklists and procedures in place for everything and everyone in your profession or work or job makes life more organised. By this approach, you can work smarter, and have better output. For achieving your goals, you do not have to be a nice guy and concede to every request which is made to you, at the cost of your own time and work. You must become an expert in the art of saying No, but in the politest manner. Written goals help us to achieve, whatever we set out to achieve. You must be clear, about what you plan to achieve. I keep a diary in my car and note books at my place of work as well as next to my bed, so that I jot down, whatever occurs to me, at all times of the day and night. Do not wait for the things to happen, but make them happen. We all have triggers, which push us about, or which make us happy or angry or sad or fearful. What motivates us or pushes us down is a reflection of our own selves. When our philosophy or view point about any subject or matter or concern is assailed or hit, we feel upset. Periodically and preferably every day, ask yourself as to what was the best or worst or most thing, which happened to you, and what lessons you have learnt from it. When any incident sparks our reaction, we need to look within. Whatever be the situation, never lose sight of your purpose. Do not be so caught up in the business of life to lose true objective and intent of your being. In the days of modern technology, experts are available in every sphere and it is a good practice to outsource some of your activities. You should not waste time on activities, which are of routine nature. Find somebody, who can do it for you on payment basis.

A good way to cross check , whether you are on the right track and are focussing on what you ought to be doing, is to write for two weeks, what you have done, all your waking hours. Do this for every three to four hours, to make things easier to track them. Then review what you have done and ruthlessly cut out all activities, which do not contribute to life and your goal. While focussing on your major goals, check whether what you wanted to do, on daily basis, has been done and not neglected. Take time out for yourself every day. You must look after yourself and your health sufficient time for to your family. Focus on whatever you are doing, whether it is meeting or talking to the people. Nobody can be know all. We can always learn from others. ■■■

21

How To Hunt For Success?

Our first impression, by others, is formed in the first twenty seconds on the basis of what we say and how we say. You must become skilled, at rating yourself, on the scale of one to ten, for evaluating your impact on others, during your interaction delivery. Your behaviour , conduct and conversation , should be such, as even to impress yourself, apart from others. Your winning over others, should be so good, that if you had to select somebody, to do business, or hire, you would select yourself.

The hallmarks of successful individuals, in the present fast moving world, is the excellence in the performance, skills and inter personal relations.

Mediocres cannot make their marks in any sphere of life. Success becomes sweeter, if we are elegant, sophisticated and courteous. Condemnation, criticism and complaining evokes a similar reaction, from the others. You have to create your own distinct brand. Other wise, you are in danger of being extinct.

The law of attraction enunciates, that "Like attracts like." In other words, the thoughts you think, the feelings you sense , the words you speak, and actions you take , have their own energy, that attracts to it more of its own sort.

Depressing and pessimistic off putting forces attract negative energies. Positive energies, invite positive powers. It is upto, each one of us, to embed the patterns of our likes and dislikes in our minds and in our scheme and technique of life. We need to let go, of the feelings and thoughts, which pull us back and drain our energy and power. By discarding the old models, in favour of optimistic and helpful designs, we attract things, of their sort to our lives. Living with negative patterns is, like running a 100 metre race, with your hands and feet tied and still hoping to win an Olympic medal. You have to make a determined effort to shed your gloomy, disheartening and usual ways of thinking, feeling and behaving. We should be careful and wise to choose our words circumspectly. Once we give a commitment, it is immoral and dishonest not to honour the same.

We should continue, to develop the ability to simplify and eliminate the unnecessary, so that, we can focus on the crucial and indispensable. The prudent and sensible people, eliminate the non essentials from their lives. You have to do, more of the essential and vital, to compensate for any failure you might have faced. No body can be poor, unless he has a poor frame of mind. The future is not, some destination or a place, to which we are heading. It is something, which we are creating as a result of our activities, right now.

One thing is certain, that in our lives, our emotions, moods and feelings, do not remain the same, all the time. Our efforts should be, to get rid of such brain waves and ideas, which are stumbling blocks. We should at all times and continually, keep on striving to fix inspiring images in our minds. This is the only way, to get rid of negativity in our lives and expel it from our minds. Letting go, is a great quality. It enables us to put behind all our past failures and unpleasant events and persons.

Only we can create a joyful life and it all depends upon us and it is upto each one of us. There is no recipe available for it, either from market, or on or off the shelf in a departmental store. You cannot make a copy of it from others. One thing is explicit, and unambiguous that any person, you come in contact, wants to be considered and treated as a very important person. This is irrespective of the fact, whether it is said overtly or covertly either by gestures or words or body language. Indeed, all of us carrying a written plaque around our necks, which says in bold letter, that "I am important and make me feel so," there is something unique in everybody. There is no buttering up or cajoling or flattering to pin point and appreciate it. Apart from pleasing others, it will yield a very rich bonus. ■■■

22

How To Do Your Best in Life?

From the lowest to the highest and from the poorest to the richest, everybody wants to be considered, as important, who has made a vital contribution, in his or her segment of life. But the problem comes when ,instead of getting down to action, most people spend a lot of time in preparation and in being mentally or physically ready to plunge into action. Whenever we are to journey, whether by plane or train, we do, everything in time to pack up our bags, keep the tickets and money handy and leave in time for the Railway Station or Airport . We do it, whether we are in a mood, to do so or are feeling sleepy or lazy.

The same approach is required, to get going and begin what we want to do, for achieving the definite chief aim of our life. You can never have perfect circumstances, for commending work, on your goal. If you go on, waiting for perfect situations, you may have to wait for the whole life. Chances are that, you may still not have the same.

The future is not, some place, or destination we are going to reach. It is something, we have to create and create right now. If there is no path to our goals or objectives, then we have to make it. The undertaking, of this very activity, will transform our life. It will bring us, near our aspirations. At the same time, we must not confuse any of our activity, with the achievement. Nevertheless, one leads to the other. At the same time, it is a fact, that both our intentions and words are a powerful means, to achieving our plans and aims. We can never be sure, or certain, that any activity, or action will give us cent percent results, at all the time or at any given time. The basic thing is, that if we want to be a success, we must complete, what we begin.

We have to take, a chance, at every step of our life. Otherwise we cannot go far. I had to travel sometimes back to Saharanpur, for an important work. But I was told that no confirmed seat was available and I would have to take a chance. I did and found a vacant seat in the Air Conditioned First Class. If I did not take a chance, I would have missed my engagement. We do not become successful, by a one time achievement. It is not a one time, proposition.

We must make success an everyday pursuit. Success is an attitude, the way, you relate to others, to your priorities, and most important, as how, you spend your time. Success is not something that happens to you. You have to make it happen. Every little detail of the system , how we tackle any task, has an affect, on our level, of success and our ability to reach it.

The way you handle small items, has a tremendous effect, on the results, you get on the big things. All big things, invariably and inevitably, are made up of lots of small things. What pains most, is the small grain or a pebble or some sand, in the shoes during our walk.

We should not neglect small things. We should use, every little step, to move towards our goal. Nothing important is gained without strain, labour and sweat. Keep doing and strive to be, the best, at your job. Use every opportunity you get, for your success and accomplishments. Your goal won't come to you. You have to move towards it. A little progress every day, will become a big progress at the end of one month, six months and one year. I make it a point, to write five hundred or more words each day. At the end of the year, there is more than enough material to publish one book.

Any major accomplishment, is the result, of cumulative efforts, put in over a period of time. When a proverb says that *'Rome was not built in a day'*, it is only stating that over a period of time, you can create eternal marvels of architecture and art. The business world is shrewd in focussing on its earning and a balance sheet every quarter, as well as comparing the same not only with the last quarter, but also, with the last year's same time quarter. Four quarters become one year and so lo and behold, the companies have made a fortune at the end of the year.

Every minute counts in life. I keep tasks ready, which can be done in ten to fifteen minutes, like returning a phone call, or even going through an article or even reading a newspaper or by writing 100 words for my next book or in decluttering my working space or my study or by clearing the junk mail, from my computer or arranging things in the order, I want them, or jotting them new ideas, which might occur. Every minute of our life, if well used, can take us, near our cherished aspiration. You have to programme yourself, to use your time well and purposefully. Indeed, I feel uncomfortable, even if I waste even a minute. You can always find a chore, which you can do in two or five or ten minutes. We may not be able to do everything, but we can always do a few things, in the time, which becomes available to us in bits. It is upto each one of us, to use every minute, in such a way, that we package all of them, to achieve anything we want to achieve. For realising our purpose, we have to make a moment to moment and day to day, commitment to it. ■■■

23

How To Accept Yourself as You are?

How others, treat you, depends upon, as to how you treat others. More than that, you get treated in life, the way, you expect others, to treat you. There are people, who get upset over minor and trivial things. If you really want to make a mark in life, make sure that you treat trifles as trifles and important things as important. We must respect other's space, compulsions and demands upon their times.

We make ourselves miserable by our expectations, as to how, others should react towards us, in any given situation, or circumstances. One thing is certain, that the world, in general is selfish and people are busy, with their own affairs or doing what they consider important and of benefit to them. You, or your problem, may not be, their priority.

But when all is said and done, nothing is ever lost by courtesy. It is the cheapest of the pleasures. It does not cost anything, but pleases, both the giver and the receiver. Courtesy is one thing, which you can not extend too much, to others. If we want, others to think highly of you, then you must extend the same courtesy to them also.

We must learn to put past behind us and stop being troubled by the things, which might have happened to us in the earlier period. All of us change, grow and develop with time . We also cultivate different perspectives on men and matters. You must become, aware of your thinking, thoughts and feelings and especially what motivates and encourages you. If something adverse has happened in your life in the past, you must get rid of it and off your chest.

There are people who might have slighted you and done something, which you felt at any given time, as humiliating. It happens to each one of us, and even I have faced it. But with the passage of time, I am able to nurture a perspective, of detachment and stand back to admit, where I was wrong and the others were wrong.

At the same time, you must be frank and honest with yourself about yourself. There is no point, in bemoaning that you wish that you were a different person. Each one of us has, both good and bad points, strengths, as well as weaknesses. Nobody is perfect.

In such a situation, you need to encourage yourself, by making a record, of what you have attained with the qualities and traits, you possess. This will not only be confidence boosting, but also give you a higher level of self acceptance, as well as highlight the positives in your life and curtail the negatives.

There are a few things, each one of us, does exceptionally well, and much better than others. In those fields our potential is unlimited and we can be the person, we want to be. We need to have perspective of the things, and problems and need not unnecessarily magnify them.

We should focus, on solving our problems, rather than concentrating on the difficulties, which may come our way. Some people feel angry, all the time, ready to erupt into emotions, over unimportant and insignificant things. Or they just snap, under too much stress, or throw a temper tantrum. It is because, they live their lives, on the edge. We need to observe those triggers, and avoid them. You can solve a problem, only if you confront it. You have to be motivated to make things happen. But what, those things should be, is for you to decide. You have to have, compelling reasons to achieve your goals. But what those goals should be is for you to decide. Without goals, there is no motivation.

Motivation is all about making things happen.

In the absence of any compelling reasons to implement the goals, there will be no motivation to achieve them.

Aim to be a winner all the time, as when winners fail ,once in while to achieve their goals, they regard the same as a temporary snag or a nuisance or at the best, an isolated incident and not a permanent stumbling block. Always be looking, for people who are success oriented or successful. Be always affirmative in your conversation. Always aim to learn from others, as to how they succeeded. Even after you do not succeed in achieving any goal, keep on observing what you have got left behind and not what you have lost. Orient yourself to count your blessings and not your adversities, troubles and tribulations. We should always remember that the vicissitudes of fortune spare nobody. But everyman is the architect of his fortune, which comes only through industry. Fortune is said to knock at everyman's door at least once in life. But most of the time, people are too busy, with their problems to hear a knock. We must remember that there is no rose without a thorn. We should look on our problems as opportunities with thorns on them. ■■■

24

How To Give Your Best to Get Your Best?

Success is highly associated, to your interactions, relations and approach to others. This also includes, your wrong exposure to others, through your wrong questions or your wrong move, all the time, in trying to find out as to what is in it for you, for any activity you do. This can be, both a bane and a boon. This is the mind-set, which all people, engaged in commerce and business adopt. It is generally embedded, both in our nature and culture. This way of thinking and attitude, can mean, that most people let go of the relationships, people and opportunities, that may apparently, appear to be unprofitable.

I have noticed that many people adopt this approach of only even greeting those people from whom they can derive a benefit right now or even later on. Others do not exist for them. In other words, they want return on their investment of even wishing others well right now.

A businessman acquaintance, once mentioned to me, that the business community, having always looked at the gains and losses of any transaction, tops in this. He was correct. A colleague, after his retirement from the Government service, told me that one of the business friends, who professed eternal friendship, not only stopped telephoning or seeing him, but even refused to take his calls. I told him that he ought to have been careful about his self-respect.

You can have no more of it, than you bargain for. For this, we should keep ourselves, free from the expectations of others. The willingness to accept responsibility for one's own life, is the first step, towards having your self-respect. It is the source from which your self-respect springs.

However, it is a fact, that all of us, cannot have the same outlook all the time. We have to be flexible in dealing with the changing world and people. Flexibility and adaptability, do not happen, just by gathering knowledge and new information. They are born, out of the mental and emotional balance. They arise, from a lack of attachment to specific outcomes, and putting care for self and others in a proper perspective. Flexible attitudes, without compromising at the core principles, can take you to new heights. What you give to life and others, comes back to you. If you meet a wall and you want to go to the other side, you have to consider the various alternatives of jumping over it or going by the left or right side, or making a passage through, by breaking a part of it, or taking another route to go to the other side.

The trouble with most of us, is that we want one solution to be the solution for all our problems. We do not look at the alternatives. We should reverse our approach, in our expectations, from others as well as the action we take in furtherance of our achievements.

We should scrutinise as to how a given situation, can help us personally and professionally.

We must be realistic, to recognise, that the only thing we can have control over, is our activities and our behaviour. We need to converge, on the opportunities, which come, in our way.

But we have to be well to deliver, as well as attain, our best in our respective fields. Wellness is not only the absence of disease, but a complete state of all-inclusive, physical, mental, and social well-being. Unless we are well and healthy, we cannot even sleep properly, or even exercise, forget about excelling, in our chosen field.

You do not need an outsider to tell you that you are not well. Your body is the first one, to give you a signal, about your state of well or ill-being. If we want to improve the quality of our lives, we have to take care and strike a healthy balance, between physical, emotional, vocational, intellectual, social and environmental segments of our lives. This is the only way, we can have enough energy. Being well in all the above sectors, is the key to our destiny and future. Only each one of us, can do the same on our own and nobody else.

Disease or illness, can really mean a recession and depression in our life. Our biggest asset, as long as live, is our health. For becoming rich, or to even to move about or work well, we need to have health and vigour. If we are sick, we cannot do much, or develop our potential fully. When we are in good health, we will generally be happy person and enthusiastic. On the days, I am indisposed or suffer from any ailment, like fever or cough, I feel miserable. I dread every minute of pain. Joy, peace and happiness totally disappear during the period of my sickness. Instead of concentrating on my work, I am pre-occupied with my disease. Most of us, take health for granted and realise its importance, when it has been adversely affected. If we are physically fit, we can live at our fullest potential and having a satisfying lifestyle.

Different people adopt different approaches to fitness. My wife goes for Yoga, whereas I prefer to go for walk and exercising. Being physically fit does not mean to have a punishing schedule. It will depend upon your age and your life style. Suffice to say, that being physically fit does required effort. But every minute, put in to keep yourself well and healthy is worth it. Poor health and poor wellness means poor quality of life. For doing anything worthwhile, we should be able to carry out the day's activities without undue fatigue and tiredness and function efficiently and effectively. Fitness does not come in a bottle. It has to be earned. Do not wait to realise its importance on the arrival of sickness. In its absence, you cannot have any worthwhile life or success in your chosen field. ■■■

25

How to Be Committed To Your Cause?

Paper work in this world is inevitable, whether you are working for yourself or for an organisation. Keeping accurate and timely record is something, which is vital for effective working. Any work requires you to keep account of your income or its source and how to balance your budget.

No work is complete unless, you have done your paper work. At the same time, we need to balance between our time and work. Though paper work is inevitable, we can always find, ways of doing things effectively and efficiently, by examining, as to how, other successful people have handled, their similar problems. We should always be learning from others, rather than making our own mistake.

In any case, mistakes should be treated as detours on the road to success. Life is a bag full, of goodies like, our good health, or our capacity, to do our jobs well. Wherever, we are, is the result of our thinking and our faith. We have the choice of taking the beaten path or make a new one.

If you do not step forward, you stay in the same place. Whatever we do, we must keep the final end, and outcome in our view. After all, it is the actions, which produce the results, we want or do not want.

Most people want a lot of things. But wanting itself is not enough. You have to want the same badly and utilise all your strength and discipline for their accomplishment. This is the only way to attain something in your life. Any excellence in any job, requires whole hearted efforts, to the exclusion of everything else, in life. The trouble is that most of us expect a lot for nothing and without putting in the requisite and the essential effort.

A colleague of mine, who retired from the Indian Administrative Service, wanted to become a writer. He asked me as to what he should do to earn a name as a top writer in the country. I told him that he would need the minimum staff of a computer expert, cum a stenographer, to whom he could give dictation. He said that he did not have time. He wanted somebody, who could write for him. He only wanted to put his signature, as he had done in service. I told him that if a clerk of a stenographer, could write well for the National newspapers, then he would not be working in that lower position. It was like wetting the clay and expecting them to be turned into bricks, by a person, who did not know anything about making bricks. To expect a person, who has spent all his life typing, to turn into an ace writer for somebody is nothing short of a miracle. Obviously, my colleague did not want to become a writer badly enough. You have to want things badly enough to attain them. Do not waste your time in doing things, efficiently, which in the first instance should not be done at all.

It may take time, to achieve your objective, but if you stick to your goal long enough and hard enough, you will finally attain the same. Our progress may be slow, but as long as we keep moving and not standing still, we will realise our goal. Remember, it is not enough to solve on problem in life. Just as there are mountains, after mountains, there are obstacles, after one obstacle. It is important and vital, to establish a reputation of reliability. If you make a promise, you must see and follow it through.

I get a lot of requests to attend programmes at various places in the country. I make it a point to make a request to send all letters to me in writing, so that I could check up my schedule before accepting any programme. Once I accept it, then I make it a point to honour it. I learnt this the hard way. Once an acquaintance made a request to me to accept a programme, which I promptly did. Then I checked up my schedule and found that the same time was committed for another engagement. I had to profusely apologise for my mistake, to get out of the second engagement.

Ethics also require that you honour all your promises.

So, for your reputation, you must check and cross check whether you are honouring all the promises made even to the humblest person. Make it a point to communicate lucidly and unambiguously.

Lack of a transparent communication can be terribly detrimental to an individual as well as your organization. You have to be watch dog, not only for yourself but also for your organisation, in yours and the organisation's overall interests.

You have to go after your dreams and goals. You have to be true to yourself, because if you are not, it will reveal. ■■■

26

How To Have A High Level of Energy?

When you have to interact with people in diverse fields, energy levels have to be very high. To maintain it, one has to have different interests, to get away from all that, which depletes it. The idea of having level of energy is to spend the same, on the things, which matters to you most. One needs to be abreast of new inventions and discoveries, which can help in this direction. Videoconferencing can eliminate stressful travelling. But travel some times, has its own admirable points, like discovering new things or places or even able to catch up on your reading during train or air journeys.

When travelling ,it will be ideal not to typecast yourself with any cuisine, as long as you can have your vegetarian or non-vegetarian preferences. It is a good idea to begin and end your day with a prayer.

Besides Sikh Religious scriptures, I also like to read the scriptures on Christianity, or Jainism or Buddhism or Islam or Geeta every day, apart from the *Granth Sahib*. In the night before sleeping , as well as before starting the day, some positive reading is a must. It really sways your thoughts. Some people do some meditation. Anything which helps you to become more efficient and a better person and encourages you to live in the present moment should be welcomed. The idea is, to do your best in your work. Always try to think positive, as positive vibes make you feel good about yourself and the world. Being positive radiates positive energy to others, including people hostile to you. Have a target to make one person happy and smiling everyday.

Focus all your energies on working hard and in achieving, whatever you have set out, to achieve. It will be a very satisfying experience. Your efforts should be, to stay healthy, as health is basic to all achievement A healthy body will enable you to work harder and for longer hours. It will make you feel more confident, and change you for the better.

Have a programme of staying healthy, by incorporating exercising in your life. Never sacrifice, your exercising regimen. I get visitors quite often and some of them turn up, when I am just going for exercise. I invite them to join me and discuss, whatever they want to say during the exercising and walking session. As most people are out of shape, they drop off soon, by cutting short their conversation, which would have gone on interminably otherwise. There are others, who meet me at functions or programmes or even during the exercise and tell me that they want to come to my place, to discuss a few things. I do not put them off discourteously, but tell them, to discuss whatever, they want straightaway. This saves me from listening to their litany of grievances later on. I tell them, without becoming impolite , that let them tell me the point, at which they want my help or guidance.

Having a friendly disposition, makes life pleasant and gives you a feeling of being, on the top of the world. Never sacrifice your relaxing and letting your hair down. Do anything, which makes you feel good, whether it is partying, reading books, meditating or seeing films. With this approach you will feel refreshed and energised.

We need to strive for continuous improvements in every walk of our life, whether it is, on office or social, or personal front. Most of the time people are rigid about their methods of working, living, socialising and even meeting others. A friend's wife, insisted on bathing her one old year baby, with cold water in severe cold in December, in Delhi, on the ground, that it is healthy to bathe with cold water. She continued doing this till her baby caught Pneumonia and was on death bed. Only after a lot of arguments, by her parents and her husband, she realised that it is not necessary to punish a baby with ice cold water in winter, so that he or she turns out to be healthy later on. It was her set thinking, which almost killed her baby, who survived due to the intervention of his grand parents.

Once I was posted in an office, where I found that I could not dictate, my letters to any body, as nobody knew stenography or typing. Any expectation that they would be typed correctly and accurately was out of question.

Conventional, conservative and fixed ideas lay down expectations, that in Government offices, that all typing work should be done by the typist or secretary or your stenographer. It was not applicable in the present context. So instead of sticking with such a person, I insisted on his transfer and got it done. His substitute was so good, that I had him transferred with me and he spent a large chunk of his service with me as my Private Secretary. At his advice, I learnt typing, when still in service. As the typing key board of the computer and the type writer is the same, the transition has been easy and very convenient. This knowledge and skill has resulted, in my having written 29 books and in honing my writing skill.

I am convinced that if we do not keep on learning throughout our lives, we are left behind. Whenever

I am faced with a problem, I think of, as to how I can solve it and not how it cannot be done. Making excuses for not doing anything and everything is the easiest thing What matters is, doing, by questioning the existing theories and practices.

This is the difference between pessimist and others. The pessimist will give all kinds of reasons and excuses as to why, something cannot be done, instead of getting into the arena and doing it. I reason, that it is better to try and get wrong results than not to try at all. Trying something is vital and is the first step in getting any outcome. Undoubtedly, better ways will be found, as we go along. We should not put off doing, under the excuse, that we are doing only 50 or 75% correctly . Starting itself will help you get past the 'stuck' up point. We can always rectify or adjust as we go along the way.

If you discover that you have made a mistake, correct it right away. Accept that mistakes are a part of life and they happen. Do what the pilots, in flying aeroplane do. Though they put their planes on auto pilot, they keep on constantly adjusting, so that the plane lands at its intended destination. It is equally true of our lives and personal self- improvement. The path to the progress and self-development is not always straight. It requires corrections from time to time. It lies in our power to do it. ■■■

27

How To Make The Most Of Outstanding Performance?

Whatever job or work you are assigned, make sure, that you know, what is expected of you. If you want to be considered valuable, the only way is, to do your job so well, that you become an asset to your organisation. Deliver more, than what is expected of you or what you pledged. You have to distinguish yourself, so that people recognise you as a super star and an excellent performer and a worker. Do not be a worker, whose boss is constantly chasing, to make sure that you are not behind the schedule. Most of the time, others assess us on the basis of information given by us.

You must also make sure that all those, who matter, know about your contribution and work. Excellent performance and work, should no be kept or remain hidden. Even otherwise, if there is no recognition, we do not feel, that we have done our best.

If you make it certain that you are performing at, or close to the top, of your occupation, nobody can prevent, you from reaching the top, inspite of the adverse and hostile conditions. The reality is that people of every gender, race and education are rising, from starter positions to top positions every day in different professions. It is their, distinguishing themselves in their respective spheres, which takes them to highest levels.

There are many means, methods, and techniques, that can take you to the top, or anywhere, you want to reach, for that matter. But you have to make certain, that you are not only, exceptional and excellent, but you continue to upgrade your skills and abilities. This is the only way, in which, you can produce consistently stunning and spectacular results.

Outstanding performance is very much and decidedly visible, not only to those, who have to assess you, but also to your peers and others. It leads you to nowhere, if you are an unmotivated, haphazard, inconsistent, and a chronic complainer. Frankly and honestly, nobody wants such people. Perhaps, even you would not want them near you.

You have to ask yourself that if you were the boss, would you invest in and hire a person, who does not live up, to your expectations and thus indirectly, is a loss making proposition, to the management.

Nobody, who is drained, directionless, pessimistic, vague, rash, scattered, critical, haphazard, distracted and hesitant can reach the top, in his work, job or profession, whether he is self-employed or working for others.

When you want to do any job, make sure, that you attend to your most important items, at your most productive schedule for the day. Then take up, your lesser important items, on the other part of the day. Schedule your items, on your time, by their value. Clearly understand, the importance of the things to be done and first focus on those items, which will give you the greatest worth, prices and consequences for your time. It is not enough, to be productive. You have to become more valuable.

You have to distinguish yourself by standing out from the herd. Good is always at the benevolence and clemency of better, as best is the adversary and a rival of the good. Both are interlinked. If you stop being better, you stop being first rate.

You are the topmost person for your career and for this you need to become a performing artist, rather than an alibi man. Basically you have to realise, that performance is everything. You must become an attractive brand, which reflects distinction, commitment and passion.

Remember that the things to be done, and in your plan never programme or reveal themselves. They do not automatically, display themselves as the next thing to be done. You have to plan them and fit themselves in the slots, which are best suited in accordance with the importance. Spend the bulk of your time on your most important tasks.

We always like to associate with people who are energetic, passionate, enthusiastic, self-directed, focused, supportive, systematic, timely and proactive. They are the ones who not only will inspire us, but will invariably make a contribution to the humanity. Indeed such people, very much inspire others so that they are propelled in the category of achievers. It is for you to join their category. ■■■

28

How To Use Your Time And Energy for the Highest Results?

No man is an island. We are all inter dependent on each other in every aspect of our lives. There are teachers, who teach us and later on our children. There are farmers, who grow vegetables, and food grains for us. There are pilots to pilot the planes to transport us. Thus there is universal support system, including those, who cheer and uplift us, though we do not consciously realise it. Life is always happening and we do not always get our ways around or realise all our wishes. Even failure has its use, as it teaches us not to repeat the same mistakes again, and consequently readjust, realign, and remap our course if necessary. This approach prevents us from reinventing the wheel. Chances are, that whatever we are trying to do, someone would have already done it successfully. It is best to at least try the methods, which had yielded the desired results to others. The world is full of experts, to guide and lead us on the path, we take to follow and tread. Using someone who has the expertise to help or guide you can make your job performance, not only easier, quicker but also first-rate.

Basically, we are accountable for what we do, and how we do and what skill or proficiency, we draw on, for all our actions. Whenever my computer gives any problem, I do not try to rectify it. I call for the services of an engineer or a programmer, who has spent his life time, in engaging himself in that profession. It is not that I have not tried to rectify the problem, myself, in my anxiety to save time or money. I have realised that in the long run, it proves counter productive and takes more time, which I try to save. You need to encourage yourself from time, for having arrived at some milestone in your life. There are two ways to be happy, one is to have all your desires fulfilled and the other is to limit your needs and desires. But most of us, like to have our desires fulfilled. We need to make it a daily habit to ensure that we are on the right track and have achieved, whatever we set out to achieve during the day. Infact, it will be a good habit to review at the end of the week and month that you have achieved your most important goal, you had set out for the specific period. But before you can do it, you have to develop the habit of scheduling. You have to be ruthless in cutting out the activities, which are a sheer waste of time and do not contribute to your long term or short term goal.

I get a lot of invitations for social functions, lectures or meetings or seminars. I am rather selective in accepting them, unless they are directly related to my objectives. I am very clear that I would spend my time, on the things, which matter most to me. Most of the invitations are politely regretted and in case of marriages or birthday celebrations, I proffer my regret and send a gift cheque. If I did not adopt this policy, then I would have no time either for my rest or recreation or the work I want to do. You have to carefully safeguard your time, against its being used by others, if you want to live by your priorities and not by other's priorities. After all, the time in life as well as our energy is limited and we should focus on, what yields us the results, we want in different spheres of our life, like health, profession or family. ■■■

29

How TO Be Unstoppable?

Vitality, vigour power, passion and purpose in life is basic to any achievement. It is a common experience, that when we are feeling listless or lack of energy or are too tired, there is hardly anything worthwhile we can do. If we want to bring out the best in us, we have to strive to be full of vigour and drive all the time. One thing is certain, that for doing anything worthwhile, we need to utilise, every minute of our life purposefully.

You must have a vision of the future, you want to create. A magnificent and a grand goal, will enthuse and motivate you, for achieving it. What vision, we should have, is for each one of us to decide. Everything depends upon us. Nobody is going to attain, our chief aim for us and hand it over to us, on a platter. It is exactly like, happiness, which we have to find, in ourselves and not in others or elsewhere. First, we have to determine our objective and then decide, the straightest road map, we shall take to realise it. We have to be focussed in whatever we do. Without it, we cannot accomplish anything worthwhile. You may chalk out rosy goals and be enthusiastic in achieving them. But without focus, you can never achieve anything worthwhile.

It is not feasible to expect or have any interruptions in our lives. We have to learn to live with them and still keep our focus.

Never lower your standards and expectations , so far as your performance is concerned. Instead raise the level of performance, not only to meet your expectations, but also to surpass them. Look forward to the most excellent and pre-eminent level of working, from yourself. After having done that, do what is necessary, to transform the same into a reality . Never hesitate to take action, as inaction, leads to uncertainty and hopelessness, which in turn generates doubt and fear. Action breeds confidence and courage. If you want to conquer fear, do not, just sit, and think about it. Go out and get done about it. Do not wait for the best decision, to take and waste your time and energy. Even the second best decision, many a time, is better, than no decision . You have to be ahead of others, if you want the people, to follow you. Leader has to lead and you can be a leader only, if you are ahead of others.

The only way, to deal with your life's challenges, is to learn, to be your own, best friend. Most people encourage others, with words of support, praise, appreciation and love. But there are very few people, who encourage themselves. Indeed, some people are, their own worst enemies, and the biggest self critics. While a majority, are at least theoretically open, to the idea of forgiving others, but they are not willing, to extend the same courtesy to themselves. A bulk of people, carry a lot of preconceived notions, on what they are capable of doing and what they cannot do. This they do, without even once trying, to crack the problem, they are facing.

This is the result of past conditioning and negative ideas ingrained in ours and their minds, that we or they, cannot do a few things ,inspite of our or their best efforts.

It is perfectly in order to pat yourself on the back and cheer yourself up, about your competencies and capabilities and be your own best friend and your own admirer.

Friends are there to see you through adversities and hard times, and who can be your own best friend than you, to yourself. When you wish to criticise and find fault with yourself, then at least, be as kind, motivating, understanding and gentle, to yourself as would be. Ask yourself as to what your best friend or friends should do, in similar circumstances.Then exactly do that yourself. Incidentally, the most practical and beautiful approach to achievement, would not work, unless you do.

Just as for maximizing our potential , we practice activities such as physical exercise, yoga, reading, therapy, mindfulness meditation. In a similar way, we need to practice activities, that enhance our mental faculties. ■■■

30

How To Make A Habit of Success?

Life gets in the way of everybody. It can be, in the form of ill health, or a financial crisis or a tragedy at the family front. We need to keep our focus, on our chief aim and aims, inspite of the difficulties, which are a part of every day life. Each one of us, should try to be a man of purpose, steadfast in his idea or ideas, and his plan or plans.

We should, all the time cherish our aspiration, dwell on the same and live it in our life and dreams, till the same, is transformed, into a reality. When difficulties come our way, we should refuse, to capitulate to them. When going gets tough, you have to be tougher to overcome the same. When somebody fails in achieving his goals, then it is worthwhile to examine, whether the failure, was due to any underlying indifference and a feeling, that the goal is not worth achieving or not worth the value or whether it was, set without applying his or her mind to the same.

Fundamentally, you have to have the strongest possible desire to attain your goal. A strong desire, will cast away any difficulties, which may come in the way to the destination of your success. Keep on making every effort, to surpass your own expectations and goals.

After realising one goal, set your sights higher, to accomplish a still, more loftier goal. Deluge your mind, with confidence building statements. You have to be, better than others, in making a mark, in your life. The only way, to be better, than others is to keep on learning and upgrading your knowledge and skills. The best way to do so, is by listening to others.

Never presume, that you possess, all the knowledge of the universe on a given subject. Consult the experts, who have spent life time, in their respective professions. This will avoid your reinventing the wheel and duplicating or triplicating or even quadruplicating your efforts. Ask those who know, the correct way to the destination, you want to reach.

Make a list of the things to be done both on daily and long term basis. After having done so, have a second look at the same, whether you can do all those things yourself or you need the help of an expert, in completing any given task. If for doing any work, you need any information, then before undertaking it, make sure that you collect the same. Do not treat learning, as a pain in the neck, but consider acquiring new knowledge as a great fun and an achievement. New skills will make you effective and acquaint you with all you need to know.

Ability, motivation and attitude, in conjunction with one another can make any goal come true. Ability is the gauge of your capacities and capabilities, motivation shows your steadfastness to your aim and attitude reveals, as to how far you are willing to go, to achieve your goal.

Keep on asking yourself questions, that lead to the direction in making yourself more competent, like , as to how I can do a better job and get the maximum out of my life and time. Each achieved goal, makes you, more confident and powerful and gives you the reassurance, that you are on the right road. Achievement of one goal does not mean perfection in life. It only reflects, that your focus was correct and efforts were sufficient. For different goals, you might have to adopt different strategies and be willing to do, if the need arises. There is no way, to ensure that one strategy, which you might have used successfully would give the successful results in tackling the next obstacle. So be open to change and in making innovations. ■■■

31

How To Live A Life Of Your Dreams?

Doing our best honestly, is the most important passion.

Every time we cheat others, we try to find justification, as well as lie, to protect ourselves and our point of view. If you want to feel worthy of success, you must have a high level of self-esteem for yourselves. Some people act or live, with an eye on, as to how others would feel. If you are always seeking, or functioning with a view, to get approval or approbation, from others, then you would not be able to do your best. As long as you feel, that you are doing the right things, do not waste your time, worrying about other's perceptions. Irrespective of the field we are in, negotiations, at all phases, is a part of human existence, as it involves resolving situations of conflicts. with someone else's interests.

Depending upon, the likely future dealings, you can decide, how much you will be willing, to adjust or play hard to get in negotiations. If you are likely to get a greater benefit, in amending your stand, then it is worthwhile to do so. Everything in life, depends upon your stake, in any issue. Whatever you might be doing, make sure that you do not lose or undermine, trust and relationships between you and others, to the extent it is possible.

You should continuously keep on organising your resources and acquiring knowledge of the field in which you are engaged in. You must be clear in your objectives, for anything you do, and what you yourself want from life, and from others. A clear vision, will enable you to be on the right direction and right road.

Only a clarity of objectives, can help you to achieve your intent. Create and recreate a vision, as to what you are doing and why you are doing it. Not only you should be focussed, but also be decisive, about your objectives. You have to work your plan and plan your work, with faith, self-discipline, and determination. All such qualities get reflected to others, without your realising that it is happening so. Individuals, naturally have great faith and confidence, in people who exude self-confidence in everything they do. They treat them as achievers in the making, who will make it big.

You must live upto your image, by walking, talking and conducting yourself as a winner. Be above board, all the time, as it is vital to keep in view not only, who is right, but what is the right thing to do.

Do not live life, according to rules and expectations of others. As children, we live by the rules laid by our parents, school authorities, religious leaders and even our neighbours. All of us deserve to be happy and live our life, on our own terms, at least after we have grown up. Nobody is under any obligation to live life, as per the expectations, or desires or rules laid by others, as long as you do not commit any crime.

If you are happy working in a particular way or in a particular station of life, that is fine, but if you are not, and if you want to change your station and take a risk, go ahead and do it. If you are sincere, things will work out beautifully. Do not be under the impression, that if you change your job and responsibility, the sky will fall or the world will collapse.

Do the things you love and have been wanting to do in your life. Follow your callings. By all means, listen to other, but still do, what you feel is right and is in line with your own taste. Do not tell yourself even in your dream, that you do not deserve, the best things of life.

If you do not believe in yourself, who will. Keep in mind, that your fears and apprehensions are in your head and imagination. It takes a lot of courage to leave the familiar and seemingly secure, to grasp the new. There is no real pleasure and happiness or even security in what is no more meaningful. There is more fulfilment in the adventurous and exciting. There is life in advancement. Change generally brings about the improvements and things we want in life.

Courage is virtue on which all other desirable qualities depend.

You cannot be creative unless you have the courage to tread new paths and dare to win. History of our lives, despite its wrenching anguish and pain, cannot be unlived, but if faced with courage, we need not live it again. ■■■

32

How to Use The Power Of Mind ?

We all deserve and have a right, to be happy and enjoy of our lives. We should never let ourselves be subjugated, to the idea, that we do not deserve the best.

Our thoughts, our words, and our actions identify and characterise us. It is they, who decide as to what we shall be or what we can achieve or what kind of life, we will live. We need to be our best, for inspiring, not only for others, but also ourselves. This approach will never misguide us. On the contrary, it will enable us, to focus on, what we want to be. Our thinking will lead us to the actions, which will transform the same into a reality, we want.

A life and work , which you love, is exhilarating and magnificent. Our work and actions should be selected carefully. They will lead us to live a life of our choice, without feeling guilty, or blame worthy. We see the positive rather than the negative, in people and situations.

For this, you may have to change, your working and lifestyle, quite often, for moving forward. We must, continually, keep on learning from our mistakes. We should use lessons, so learnt for making improvements to move forward. Each failure, should move us closer to success. Even if the progress is at a slow rate, we must continually seek to act, for reaching our desired goal. Even if you take two steps forward and one backward, it is still a progress, however slow it may seem. Only you and you, can create the life, you desire. Each one of us, has a unique talent and skill. Our progress depends upon discovering it and capitalising on it.

History is replete with the instances of the most notable winners, who usually faced, heartbreaking obstacles before they succeeded. Their success was due to the fact, that they refused to give in and accept defeats. Even in our ordinary day-to-day living, most often, we have to strive more than once to achieve our aims.

In metropolitan areas, it is normal and usual to be caught up in traffic snarls. But nobody abandons his car in despair even if he or she has to wait for hours. Ultimately, everybody makes to his destination. It is exactly, this kind of approach, we need to have, for realising our ambitions, in our day-to-day life. Our approach should be, to refuse to become disheartened and dejected by our defeats.

Of course, this comes at a price of a lot of determination, dedication, self-discipline, and effort. You should not indulge in any activity or work, or association or for that matter, anything, which depletes your energy. The higher your energy level, more efficient will be your body, and more productive, you will be in your work and job.

It is human nature to think highly of ourselves and judge others, by the standards of what we have already and in relationship to our own capabilities. Nobody, including an astrologer, can predict your future, except by what you do now. Your degrees of happiness should either to be happy or very happy or about to become the happiest person in the world.

Do not entertain any other condition or classification. Make it a habit to end yesterday, with yesterday only. Let not its worries or problems be brought over, to, today. Otherwise, the same will plague to day also, as they did yesterday.

There is no, such thing, as permanency in life. Things, situations and people change and unless we do, with them, we will be left behind. If you are successful today, then it is not necessary, that you would be successful tomorrow also, unless you are constantly working for it. Sitting on your laurels, is the surest way to be left behind. There is no recipe for success, at all times, in all situations. This approach is a sure guarantee of decay, degeneration and break down. We need to keep on reinventing ourselves all the time and in all the situations. Even if you are doing well, never fall to temptation, of sitting back and relaxing. Not only, you have to be on the right track, but also keep on running the race of life, to avoid being run over.

A sign of growth, in your life is when you improve upon, what you did or achieved in the past. Growth is not possible without change and both are inextricably linked. Keep on questioning yourself, whether there is a better way of doing, what you are doing now?

Remember, that no internet and no mobile phones, would have come into existence, but for the question, that the scientist posed to themselves for finding better and instant methods of communication. All of us have a tendency to protect and stick to our methods of working, living and functioning. We become defensive, when some body criticises us or asks us to change.

If we want to grow, then we need to look at our performance afresh ,or hire an outsider, or a consultant, who can give an unprejudiced advice and assessment. There is always a better way, a more efficient approach, a more effective system for doing things. You have to let go of past mistakes and past unproductive decisions, in favour of better decisions and more productivity. If we are successful in any venture, we should continue building our success, instead of just being satisfied. You have to be a success not only yesterday, but also today as well as tomorrow. ■■■

33

How To Utilise The Secrets of Successful Delegation?

However, efficient and hard working, we might be, we cannot do everything. Successful leaders, in every walk of life, are the masters of delegation. Delegation serves, to get the task completed faster and at a low cost of time and money, if done properly. It also enables, the delegator to save his time, which he could spend elsewhere to complete some other more vital tasks.

It also enables the delegatee to develop his confidence and capabilities. However, before a job is delegated, the delegatee should be clearly told, as to what out come, is expected of him and in what time frame.

He should be fully apprised of his boundaries of work and whose help or guidance he can rely upon, He should also be informed, as to when and how he can involve higher levels of authorities to sort out his difficulties, which he cannot handle himself. But at the same time, the delegator, should make sure that under this guise, there is no upward delegation.

Wherewithal and means include amongst other things, time, equipment, supplies, space, money, and manpower. When choosing to delegate, you must know, well in advance, the level of skills and competence, of the delegatees. Selecting the right person, for any delegated job is the first step in getting the best results from allocating the task to others.

Delegation works best, when it is done in favour of the people, who are closest to the work. They are best suited, as they have the most intimate knowledge of the detail of everyday work, at the ground level. This also increases, the workplace efficiency, and helps to build up them.

Delegation can be effective only, if we can match the person with the appropriate skills required for doing a job, which you may like to delegate. Sometimes, you may not be able to find a person, who has all the skills you are looking for. In that case, select a person, who has the most vital skills and then make the corresponding match.

If the delegated task, is to be done by a team, it is equally vital, to know the competencies, of each member of the team and which of them, can handle some tasks independently and in which part of the task, they need guidance. The team must be communicated concrete, measurable, concise and deliverable objectives. You must let the delegatees know your expectations clearly.

When you assign a task, be very clear about the deliverables you expect. Quantify your expectations, as much as possible. As a minimum, you need to communicate the "what" and the "when".

It is ideal to give a deadline for completing a task. But a realistic deadline, should preferably, be mutually agreed upon, between the delegatee and the delegator. A deadline, makes all concerned, responsible for completing the task, as per schedule. The delegator should let go of details of how the work will be done. He should focus only on results. This should be left, to the individual delegatee or the team as the case may be to take care of the same. They should be encouraged to show creativity, to solve their problems, with the ultimate idea of showing expected results. This will also develop the skills and talents of the delegatees and prepare them for taking over the leadership later on.

However, at the same time, you must have some arrangements, of feedback, from the delegated. It can be, either by phone or e mail or a written report, at a pre-determined timings. Never commit the mistake, of delegating a task and forgetting about it, till the deadline timings. You must have mid term review points.

If a job has been well done, then be lavish and hearty in your appreciation and admiration. The delegatees would also like to have a feedback, as to how they have performed. Even the star performers need to be appreciated that they have lived upto, what was expected of them. If for some reasons the delegatees cannot complete the job or tasks assigned, tell them, to be honest, instead of doing a shoddy job. A job well done earns praise from all quarters and is the hallmark of successful individuals and organisations. The simple truth is that if you want to do more, you must delegate more, to get more jobs done from others. The whole idea of delegation or 'stop doing yourself' is to free up the time of the delegator, for doing more important work, instead of on routine tasks. ■■■

34

How To Reap Double Benefits in life?

We all make mistakes and later on wish, that we had not made it.

Nobody is mistake proof. The important lesson to be learnt, in such a situation is as to how we can benefit from them. Once we burn our fingers, by putting them in the fire or touching a burning or a hot object, we rarely repeat the experience. Even the animals and children know that walking on the precipice of a mountain, may mean their fall and certain death.

Our failures are our warning signal. The biggest challenge is, to decipher and work them out to our advantage. This is the major ordeal, we face, in our day to day life.

We should learn to treat our mistakes as our principal and foremost know-how. Mistakes are the indicators and warning signs, as to where we need to rectify and suitably modify our approach to any predicament or impasse. Instead of being remorseful about our mistakes, we should treat them as experience. Failure or success is a matter of discernment, opinion and assessment. If something, unwelcome has happened, due to a mistake committed by you, then take stock, to discover as to why, a particular outcome came about. You do not have to damn yourself for any slip-up.

Instead, evaluate it and take constructive steps, to avoid the same in future and move on. Finally and ultimately, you are responsible as to what has come about. The only precaution, you should take, is not to make the same bloomer and lapse again. Whatever we do in life, and whatever choices we make, there will always be rough patches. Learn from the choices or options, you exercise, in doing your chores. Many a time, we notice that what we conceive as a mistake or a misfortune today, might in hindsight appear to be the best thing to have happened.

My late father, Mahant Kartar Singh, was keen that I should study and make something of my life. Though difficult, he managed to spend Rs. 20 per month on me, for my school education and stay in the hostel, in Ferozpore from 1953 to 1955. He was a matriculate himself, which was a big achievement in 1937. He saw to it, that I went to the best college in Punjab at that time. Seeing others succeed in All India Services Examination, I also appeared and got selected in the Indian Police Service.

My late mother was against my going out to study. She wanted me to open a shop and become a grocery salesman. She was right, at that time, as the money was scarce. She did not say openly, but the fact was that my parents could hardly afford my school and later on college expenditure. But what appeared to be a miscalculation at that time, tuned out, to be, the best thing to have happened not only to me, but also to my family and made my village proud of me. What appeared to be a mistake of spending money on my education, turned out to be a blessing in disguise.

Next time, you make a mistake, smile and ponder about the possibility of its being a blessing in disguise. It is only our mistakes, which illustrate and confirm, as to what needs improving in our lives. Without mistakes, we would not know, what we should work on, to improve the quality of our life and work. Mistakes give us, another chance to get and become better. They are indeed the portals of discovery. Falling down due to mistakes is no sin or crime, but staying there, it is.

If you have made mistakes, even serious ones, there is, always another chance for you. What we call failure, is not the falling down but the staying down.

Mistakes are the portals of discovery. We should not waste our time either in regretting or ruminating over our mistakes, rather than look forward to a glorious future. The past cannot be changed. But all of us, can do something about the future. What we should do, with the future lies in our power. We should laugh at our mistakes and move on . It is the greatest mistake in life, to continually fear making mistakes. The only person who makes no mistakes, is the one, who does nothing.

Mistakes are a truth and a reality of life. It is the response to them, that matters. Once Theodore Roosevelt, the former President of USA said; "It is neither the critic who counts, nor the man who points out how the strong man stumbled, or where the doer of deeds could have done better. The credit belongs to the man who is actually in the arena, whose face is marred by dust, sweat and blood, who strives valiantly, who errs and comes, short again and again, who knows the great enthusiasm, the great devotion, and spends himself in a worthy cause, who at best knows achievement and who at the worst if he fails at least fails while daring greatly so that his place shall never be with those cold and timid souls who know neither victory nor defeat". ■■■

35

How TO Develop And Use Discretion?

All of us, want many things in life. Our expectations vary from time to time , place to place and person to person. The real skill and art, consists in, harmonising all of them.

It is not the wittiest or the most educated or the bravest, who carries the day , but the most discreet. There are many wonderful and shining qualities, which many men possess. But, the most worthwhile quality, is discretion. How you interact and react, with others, is a measure of your intelligence and use of discretion.

The quality of being discreet, can be described, as the wise conduct and management; cautious discernment, especially, in propriety and self-control; prudence; circumspection and concern.

I have been in very tricky situations, but the timely use, of discretion has saved the day for me. Once in a meeting, with the Prime Minister, I noticed that the Prime Minister was quoting some facts and figures, which were totally different from the actual ones. He looked at me, to confirm that whether what he had said ,was right.

I slightly nodded to express my agreement with him. But as I did not want him to be faulted with, I sent him a slip, saying that if deemed proper, he could add, that the situation can change, from day to day and what holds good may not be good enough, for tomorrow. Since he had a lot of confidence in me, he said, the figures could be subject to correction from time to time.

Later on he asked me, as to why I wanted him to say, what I had written on the slip. I explained that the figures could be wrong in matter of days, and I did not want anybody to fault him on that score. He appreciated my discreet and quite intervention.

Discretion is both the salt and sugar of life. One preserves and the other sweetens it. Without discretion and use of proper language, the relations sour and sometimes rupture.

Discretion is cultivated, by weighing pros and cons, of any given action or reaction. Discretion is the highest prudence and is vitally useful both in social, personal and political relationships.

We need to exercise discretion not only in our day to day life, but also in matrimony. If we are not discreet in consuming food, we may be choked to death by it. There are no set rules as to how to cultivate discretion. Injudicious, and indiscreet defence, of even the best cause, can harm it. In discretion, if we are masters, we sometimes need to be blind and if we are servant, then we need quite often, to be both blind and deaf . Even if you have great ability, and no discretion, in use of it, you may come to grief or not attain the desired results.

Discretion is needed every day, in almost all activities of our lives for making a right decision. Discretion also involves, sometimes, taking one step back, so that you can take two steps forward.

Discretion is equally required for making laws and implementing them. Many a time, for greater good, the best of decisions have to be reversed, on popular demands, or for dealing with unique situations. To save lives, often the Government had to release terrorists or Maoists, as a barter, to save lives, in the interest of greater good.

Many decisions to tax or reduce tax have been taken, by the Government, when the coalition allies did not support the decisions. Discretion in decision making can be analysed from the choices and flexibility available. We must be discreet in speaking to others, as speaking agreeably is more than eloquence.

Shakespeare says on discretion through a buffoon character Falstaff:

"To die is to be a counterfeit, for he is, but the counterfeit of a man, who hath not the life, of a man; but to counterfeit dying, when a man thereby liveth, is to be no counterfeit, but the true and perfect image of life indeed. The better part of valour is discretion, in the which better part I have saved my life."

In other words, Falstaff is saying that he has hidden, or even played dead, when on a battlefield, in order, to avoid any personal danger.

These days, the phrase denotes that caution is a smarter policy to adopt than hot-headedness. It is better to be prudent than merely courageous. It is something like looking before you leap. Charles Churchill put it in poetic form: "Even in a hero's heart, Discretion is the better part".

A sound discretion, is not so much shown, by never making a mistake, as by, never repeating it. Other requirements of discretion are to speak less than you know. Knowing, when to keep your mouth shut, is more important than opening it at the right time. Be discreet in advising others. Neither give advice nor salt, unless you are asked for it. Discretion is a very valuable quality in a working place. Indiscreet comments can harm the reputation of an organisation, as well as of the individual workers. We need to develop, maintain and enhance, discipline, discernment, discrimination. detachment and discretion in life, for improving the quality of our lives and work. The most important thing in life is to separate the chaff from the grain and pick and choose the best. We need to make a good judgement in our daily dealing with the people, so that we can select the best as our associates. ■■■

36

How To Conduct Small Talks?

Small talk is a harmless and a safe, way to break the ice with the strangers, or people we come across on social occasions, It may or may not have any solid content, but is practised on social and other occasions quite often. It includes non personal and non controversial contents and subjects, like weather, the current social and political style of celebrities or the traffic jams on the roads or the current economic or political state of affairs in the country or poor banks or postal services.

It is practised, with the people, we come across every day, but hardly know them, like the fellow morning or evening walkers or co-travellers in lifts or while waiting for the public transport. I come across, fellow customers in departmental stores and with them, my small talk is of a smile, as with the salesmen at the check out counters. Small talk is impersonal and does not attack anybody individually.

But for the small talks, many social functions and parties would be a disaster, for the people attending the same, as where mostly the guests hardly know each other. It is a staple food, at the parties, where the guests only know the host, independently. Small talk breaks the uncomfortable silence. It is both non committal and non controversial. Examples of small talk is greeting each other and inquiring about the family. Small talk is a great social vehicles, and without its use at the appropriate time, we would appear to be rude, impolite, and discourteous. We need to use it, for most of the time, like when travelling with fellow passengers by air or train, when visiting hospitals and thanking doctors and nurses for attending to our needs and problems, or even thanking others, for giving us the right of way. Small talk has its place in our lives and especially when you are stuck as to what to say next. Making small talks can be a challenge. It needs as much preparation, and confidence, to make small talk, as it does for doing anything else worthwhile. For instance, whenever I go for any social function, I make sure that I have full information about the occasion and the type of people, who would be present. I go through my own compilation of joke books or good quotes, so that at the appropriate time, they could be used. I do not over do it, and make the whole conversation look like a spontaneous reaction, to any remarks or a repartee. Small talk practice can be done, with anybody, we may come across, like our neighbour, fellow workers, or the people we come across, both officially and socially. Read the newspapers and magazines on current affair, as well as acquire knowledge, on any other subject, which may come up, for discussion, or which might be of interest to the circle, or people you are likely to meet. Keep a journal, in which you can note the funny stories, quotes or other interesting anecdotes, which you can use during small talks. Being a good listener will give you a good cue, as to what part of the small talk will sell or would be of interest to others. Always keep on trying and learning some thing new, so that you can expand your horizons and become versatile in small talks. Keep in mind your company and do not use, vulgar or obscene stories to attract the attention of others. Do not use anything, which might appear, offensive, odious or unpleasant to others or be distasteful or disgusting. Humour and confidence are valuable assets for small talk. But the humour should be clean and not bawdy. Do not monopolise all the conversation, while doing small talk. Small talk at times, can be crucial in making or breaking personal relationships. Think before you participate in small talk, as to what you are going to say and what effect, it will have on others. Conversation is not a one way process and does not happen in vacuum. In the small talk effort should be to convey the impression, that you are both confident and intelligent. Do not show any emotion or passion or any prejudice, when doing small talk. Small talk on social occasions is not a forum for serious discussion or putting loaded questions or for showing people down. Keep a smile on your face, when doing the small talk. A happy and a smiling person is welcome anywhere, as he or she spreads joy and exuberance. While doing small talk, make people feel good about themselves, to put them in a good mood, which will make your conversation with them easier and smoother. Never start an argument, while having a small talk and avoid any topic, which may lead to any controversy. Paying compliments even on innocuous matters like dressing up or pose or conducting one self is the safest approach in small talks. The idea of any small talk is not to prove any particular stand or a point of view, but to socialise. ■■■

37

How Not To Be Stuck Up in A Quagmire?

We can bring about any miracle in our lives, by a determined spirit, industry and perseverance. There are, inherent qualities of leadership, in all of us, which have been smothered, over a period of time. As children, we are persistent, in getting what we want and do not ordinarily give up.

But a crescendo and pattern of NO, Don't, and Can't, No! Don't do this, Don't do that, You can't do this. You can't do that, Don't ask silly questions, deprogrammes and destroys our creativity.

Unfortunately, this pattern started at home, continues in our schools and other educational institutions. Later on, it is repeated in the profession, jobs we may be doing. The result is, that instead of thinking for ourselves, and becoming creative, we get used, to being, the order obeyers of the hierarchy.

However, it is also essential, to maintain some discipline, in any organisational functioning. Nonetheless, if we want, to be leaders, in our walks of life, we need to be clear, that leadership and arrogance do not go together. People generally hate arrogance and showing off. You have to be interested in others and their problems, before you can lead them.

Effective leadership involves effective communication. But effective communication is possible, only if you are a good listener. Good listening is also a way of showing interest in others.

SWOT, which denotes Strengths, Weaknesses, Opportunities, and Threats, is an equally useful tool for individuals, as it is, for big organisations . Its appropriate use, can lead to both our personal, as well as, professional development.

It is best, to make an inventory, of our strong as well as weak points. Nobody, in this world, is without both strong and weak points, which enable him or her, to cash on or miss the opportunities, which life offers.

My own strong points, apart from many others, include persistence, punctuality and giving my best, to whatever is required to be done. My weak point is, that quite often, I am a victim of impatience and cannot stand boring people or fools. But I realise, that you have to accept, the good with the bad and the best. So often, I put up, with what might not be the best alternative, but only as a compromise.

I try to focus on my strengths rather than weaknesses, so that I do not miss any vital opportunity, which might come my way. I use my past accomplishments, to boost my strengths, which can be done, by everybody. It must be borne, in mind, that in day to day life, we all meet challenges, which can be, as small a thing, as a bounced cheque, or change in job, or a health or a family problem. Resilience, is the best way, to bounce back from any adversity. No life is, without problems. It does not pay to rue over them.

At the fag end of my career, I was transferred from the post of Director CBI, to an inconsequential post, by the then Prime Minister, when I refused to carry out his oral orders, to bail out an influential criminal. This happened, when I was abroad, for an Interpol meeting.

On returning to India, a Press man asked me, at the airport, as to what was my reaction, to the transfer, which many felt, was humiliating. I smiled and said, "Wonderful. Things could not have been better, as it is the same highest salary in the government and no work".

Lamenting would not have improved the position, but only added to my misery. Even in the new job, I stayed committed and engaged myself with zest, in the humdrum of official life. I took new things coming my way, with the approach, of looking forward and not looking behind me. I took control of the situation, which is the opposite of powerlessness.

Any problem facing us is not the end of the world. While we cannot change the world, but we can effectively handle, the events, by dealing with them, in a constructive way.

We must, continuously protect ourselves, from influence of negative, depressing and pessimistic people. We should not react to hardships and debacles, vengefully, like a wounded prey.

Failure is not falling down, but being reconciled, to it, and staying down. In any case, there is no point, in bashing yourself, over a single failure. To cope up, with any hardship, it is vital, to stifle any tendency, to blame yourself or other people. When you blame yourself, you are shying away, from the responsibility, for your actions and life. It is better, to ask yourself, as to why a particular thing has happened and what actions, skills, talents, or resources, you need to turn the tide.

We all, normally tend, to take credit, for good things in life, which have come to us, as a result of our efforts. Similarly, we should, also be and are equally responsible for our troubles and fiasco. Instead of pondering on adversities, we should focus on the results we want.

Mostly unconsciously and quite often consciously, we indulge in self talk. Many a times, self talk acts as a damper, which results, in our talking ourselves, out of the results, we want. It is a continuous self chatter, in our brains, about our thoughts, beliefs and judgements about men and matter. Often, we do not realise, that we are doing the self talk. Our effort should be, to take more care, of what even we remotely auto suggest to ourselves, as it invariably affects our moods, emotions and hence, our actions. Never condemn or down play yourself in your self talk.

We should be life long learners, and never hesitate to learn and review our failures, as to what lead to them. We have to own up our set backs, as we own up our accomplishment . In this process, any thing that helps, like the self talk or resilience or the support of the others, should be used, so that we can get the outcome , we want. ■■■

38

How To Make A Difference in The world?

Most people want to make a difference in the world, for the better. Think before you act. Most of our problems, come from speaking, off the cuff. If we think, before we speak, we are likely to do more right and less wrong. This will benefit every body. Instead of discouraging, let us, make it a habit, to encourage others. This will have, a multiplier effect. Remember, that we ourselves need encouragement in all what we do. All of us like people who buttress and buoy.

Many a time people succeed, because somebody, encouraged them, at the right moment. As a Young District Police Chief, with just six years of service, I received a letter of appreciation and commendation signed personally, by the Chief Secretary, to the Government of Karnataka. It was a letter, which I remember by heart till this day, commending my efforts, in expelling overstaying foreign citizens out of the country.

I was so elated, with excitement, that I could hardly sleep in the night. It encouraged me to do my job, with still more dedication, sincerity and honesty. It set me, on the chain, to appreciate my subordinates, whenever, any of the police officers, working with me, did some extraordinary work.

It built a world of faith and trust for me, where I could , achieve more and more, with the other's help. I have never grudged helping and appreciating others. It has earned me, the love, affection and respect of the people appreciated. I have also noticed with a long service experience, whether high or low, everybody craves and desires, appreciation and encouragement. Whenever I have appreciated even the Prime Ministers of the country, they have always nodded approval or smiled, indicating that they liked what I had said.

One of the most beautiful and best gifts, we can give, to anybody, is that of encouragement. It does wonder, in crossing the thresholds, which, we may not, have otherwise, attained, on our own. But it has to be, a genuine encouragement and not something phony or undeserved.

There were some colleagues of mine, who would show to their bosses, that they had done everything, including the work done by others, including the subordinates.

I have never tried to claim credit for the job done by others, as it is nothing less than theft. Another quality, with which I made a difference to the world, was that I showed respect, politeness and courtesy, to all, irrespective of their position and station of life. A colleague complimented me, by saying that my behaviour has been the same, even with the humblest, even when I occupied some of the most important positions in the Government. Showing respect for others, demonstrates good manners also. It is the respect, which begets the respect. While doing my job, my approach was one of the professionalism, total devotion and passion for my job. I love, whatever I have to do and I do not and did not treat any assignment as a pain in the neck.

Another way of succeeding and making a difference in life and to the world, is to start, with the belief, that you are going to succeed in whatever, you are doing or do. I do not even think of failure. Even if I fail, in something I want to do or I undertake, I do not treat, it as a final failure, but a temporary set back, which would be overcome in the next effort.

I have been able, to make a difference to my life, work, and the world, through the technique of examining all possibilities and taking advance action, in plugging all the loopholes and take steps, before hand, to obviate any possibility of failure, in all ventures, I have undertaken.

Instead of finding reasons, as to why I cannot succeed, I try to discover the reasons, as to why I can.

I do not bother, as to how many people say, that something cannot be done or how many have failed in attempting to do so. I know that whatever I am doing, is my first attempt. If for any reason, one of my dream does not fructify and breaks into thousands pieces, I am never afraid, to start from fallen pieces, and begin again.

The world is round and the place, which may seem to be the end, in any venture, could also be, its beginning. If we want to make difference to the world, we cannot expect victory, all the time, but at the same time expect, no defeat. We have to plan for victory.

The first step is the intention, which only can lead to commitment, with our heart, soul and very essence. You must dream big.

Do not limit yourself, with small minded thinking. Many great things, have been attained by the people, who refused, to give up, on their aspirations. Choose one thing at a time and focus on it, Do it well and finish it, instead of, taking up, too many missions or assignments. The best illustration is that of sportsmen, who take up, only one item, like running, hockey or football and master it.

You have to stay focussed on whatever you are doing, irrespective of, what is happening around you. Focus is allied with persistence and one cannot do one, without the other. Enjoy, whatever you are doing.

An ancient proverb says, that "To everyone, is given the key, to heaven; the same key opens the gates of hell". It is upto each one of us, to make our optimism come true. We all meet failures from time to time and feel wronged. The same are nothing, unless we continue, to remember them. What is possible, is, what we, will. Falling is not bad in life, as long as, while getting up, you pick up something.

You have to carry your own attitude and happiness with you. We get in life, what we give to it. Even if life, in your quest, for making a mark in the world, gives you a lemon, make a lemonade, by being an optimist. There is no use, of being, anything else. You do not have to go to fortune teller, to know your fortune. Remember, that you can be the good fortune, with your own efforts and enterprise and can make a difference to the world. ■■■

39

How To Manage Your Life and Work, Through Meaningful To Do List?

We all want to accomplish more and more in our lives and that also smoothly. But the truth and undeniable truth is, that we have to work on it and for it. You do not need a lot of investment, except in paper and pen and some exclusive time to do it. There is, no right, or wrong a way. You can use any method or format, with which you feel comfortable, while planning what you have to do.

Even if you have prepared a do list for the day, it does not mean, the end of the work. As the day spreads out, you will find new items claiming your attention. Whatever be our station in life, we will always have umpteen things to do, than when we started preparing or prepared the DO LIST.

My own approach is, to list, as many things, as I have to do during the day. It might be, as small a thing, as buying a tooth pick, or a tooth paste or paper, for my computer printer, or drawing money or depositing a cheque or returning a phone call or meeting somebody.

Be sure to list everything, you need to accomplish. The more you can, account your self for and list it, the more smoothly, your day will run. It will ensure that you will need less to remember. After making a list, prioritize tasks in the order of urgency, giving the highest priority to the most important ones, and the lesser one, to less important ones.

The first priority, should be, your mandatory engagements or appointments like your business meeting, or attending to your official programme or doing the things, around and in the office and our working place. For some mandatory work, can be dropping or picking children coinciding with the school timings. All of us, have the most productive or less or least productive time, during the course of the day. We should use, as a rule, our most productive time, principally, for our most vital and demanding tasks. Schedule, an easy job after a difficult one, or a long task after a short one to keep yourself stimulated.

Apart from the Daily Do List, keep a list, of your ongoing tasks and projects, you need to accomplish, as a part of your life goals or long term goals. A Do list should not be, inconsistent with, your long term or life goals. Infact, it should be a step towards achieving the same.

It is equally important to have some time for your entertainment and leisure, which could be in the form of reading a book or watching a video or a family outing, once in a while. If you feel, that you are off the track, and consider, that at the end of the day, you did not accomplish much, then it is time to do introspection.

You will discover, because it is so, as you had, too many distractions and too many unimportant things taking your time and pulling you in different directions. For starter, it will be best to keep only five items on the list and keep them crossing off ,after you finish them. When working, we should either have no stress or at the best have lowest possible stress level. It is because stress affects your efficiency and the quality of output of the items, you are focussing on.

With the availability of the internet connectivity, we can use email or other web based tools to remind us, as to what is to be done for the day. Of course, for this, you have to be connected to the internet and make entries in the computer, as to, what engagements you have on any given date.

You can use a diary or even loose sheets for the day. The advantage, of using a diary, is that in our country, due to the lack of electricity, interconnectivity, means no internet and hence, no reminder service.

I use a mixture of TO DO LIST tools, like the internet, wall calendar, diary, and my I Phone. It does take time to make entries, but this approach, leaves no scope for missing any programme. One of the duties, of my Private Secretary is, to make sure, that all entries are made on the wall calendar and the relevant programme given to me on the morning of the programme. He also makes a photocopy of any communication or invitation and gives it, to my driver, so that he can take me to the relevant place in time, in case, any engagement requires my presence outside my residence.

A friend of mine uses PDA or a Personal Digital Assistant, which he always carries with him. But all such gadgets require integration with the calendar. Microsoft outlook is another great electronic tool for attending to TO DO LIST.

Another friend uses sticky notes, where he can see them, as to, what tasks, are to be done for the day. I find them rather messy, but they are, one sure way, of not forgetting as to what you have to do. It must be borne in mind, that a TO DO LIST, is only a reminder service, and not a substitute for doing the work. It is up to, each one of us, to design our life, the way, we want it to be. A convenient excuse, given by many is that they do not have the time. The truth is, all of us have the same amount of time, that is a total of 24 hours in day.

Some people always have the time, to do the things they want to do and are vital for their life and career and other use the excuse of constant demands and pressure of other responsibilities. It is not hard, to find time, by freeing yourself of the unnecessary, fruitless, unproductive, self imposed stipulations, meeting and social responsibilities in our lives.

I get a lot of invitation to become member of various groups, or join sites like Face Group. Not only I find them futile, but also an ineffective use of time. Instead of frittering, away my time, in interacting with faceless strangers, or even mere acquaintance, I find it wiser, to use the same time, for either reading a book or writing some piece, for a newspaper or a magazine.

For finding time, for the things, we want to do, we really need, to have a close look, on our life and methods of working, regularly, so that we can either reduce or minimise, or drop, waste of time activities, out of our lives. The time so saved, can be used, for doing what you think, is going to improve our life or the quality of our existence or for doing the things, we love to do. Remember, that your life is your own and you can make of it, what you want, and do the things, you want. To DO LIST is one way of reaching your goal. It is upto you to live, by your own priorities, rather than other people's wishes or concerns or suggestions. ■■■

40

How To Create Your Own Paradise Anywhere?

An important rule, to be always, borne in mind, is to give full time and complete concentration to whatever we are doing. It should be our first priority. Otherwise, we would not be doing justice to any job. Everyday of our life, we should ask ourselves, whether there is anything significantly different, about our life, than it was yesterday or even last month or last year, or whether it is the same, as it was earlier?

Also ask yourself, whether you have been able to make the changes you wanted in your life. You must ask yourself, whether your motivation level, is continuing to be the same, or whether your enthusiasm has waned. If the answer is, in the negative, then you must introspect, as to what you can do, to rectify the situation.

Never berate yourself, if you are behind your agenda. Instead celebrate your achievements, in life so far. Move on, to put your life on right track. Always bear in mind , that the thoughts, both positive and negative, and the words you use, play a tremendous part, in shaping the person you are and what you become in life. The kind of questions, you ask yourself is the type of life, you lead. Our questions set off their own set of answers, which in turn lead to certain actions or inactions which are reactions, prompting equal results. If you ask, backward pulling questions, you naturally get disempowering answers. On the other hand, if you ask yourself, questions, as to, what you can learn from any given experience, or how you can empower your life, and get on a better path, or for what you are grateful in life, you get empowering answers.

You can begin, with describing yourself, in glowing terms, in your mind, at least. It need not be shared with others, if you feel, that others would pull you down. Your effort should be to build yourself up all the time, by using, meaningful adjectives, to describe yourself.

You should not make your work a pain in the neck. In its place, make sure, that you are never seriously depressed, though it is not always possible to avoid bad periods in life. You can be happy even if you are depressed, if you have a positive attitude. You can see some positive points in every situation. Never even remotely think that any problem, whether of health or finance is going to last for ever. Life is a cycle, in which ups and downs are a part of life, as long as we live. It is not, to deny the existence, of any negative aspects. However, it does not help in any way to dwell on it. Every situation, whether big or small in life has a positive side.

Last month, I went for two dinners, at the same five star hotel, in Delhi. The positive side of going, was that I could meet a few old friends, living in different parts of Delhi. The negative side was, that it involved spending nearly four hours, including the journey time. As long as we live, we need some socialisation activities, as the old saying says, that all work and no play makes Jack a dull boy. Here I can replace, Jack with Joginder. I had done a mental calculation and discovered that it would be better to go for dinner. But I made it a point, to spend, not more than one hour at both the dinners and then was driven back, by my driver.

It is better to face any issue squarely, instead of waiting for the situation to aggravate and amplify. Get, what is annoying you most, out of your way. Nothing frustrating goes away, because you sleep over it. On the contrary, it can lead to unhappiness, depression, anxiety and stress.

We should at the same time, focus on happy thoughts and develop a habit of expecting the best. If we work at it, we will get it. We generally tend to fulfil, what we expect from ourselves. You do not have to live upto other people's expectation, nor you should expect others, to live upto yours. You should not base your living on other people's desires or suggestions, unless you also agree with them.

Of course, your own aspirations and yearning should be higher, than you expect. Be a willing worker, for your ambition. It is a fact, that a thing becomes easy, when you want and work hard.

We all live in the same world and under the same sky. But as we are made differently, we do not have the same horizon, in the way we look at the same things.

Nothing comes in life without sweat and it is upto each one of us to make ourselves happy, or strong or miserable by our approach. But one thing is certain, that the amount of work is the same. Good fortune only comes to those, who expect it and it runs away from despair and gloom. A few months back, when I was returning from Kathmandu, Nepal, my plane was one hour late and while going from Delhi, it left two hours late. I simply did all the pending work, on my laptop, by plugging in the nearest power outlet. I realised that grumbling and complaining would not serve any purpose. Indeed, I looked upon the waiting time, as the time gained and prepared myself for the lecture scheduled for the evening. We can create a paradise, at any place, depending upon the way, we look at things. If you expect the best, you would find nature and circumstances, literally conspire to bring the best to you. ■■■

41

How Not To Back off in Life?

It is imperative, to use your time well. One way, you can do it, is by celebrating life and the present time, in your life and by developing lasting relationships. Life is a continuing affair. We should, equally enjoy the journey, before reaching the destination.

Any destination is not the end of an ambition, because after we reach one destination, we strive for another aspiration . We should get rid of past burdens, as they, otherwise ,would drag us down and pull us back.

We should forget past and move on or in other words, use 'Forget the Past and Move On' method. We should treat every day as a new day. We need, to constantly renew, our motivation, which in simple language, means a motive for any action we do. It could be anything, we perform, relating to our profession or job, or business or family or our hobby or hobbies.

We should invest our time, in the things, which are important to us, in all our life's activities. This approach is the greatest asset, anybody can have. There is no finality, at any stage in our lives, in which we can say, that we have learnt, all that is, relevant to our calling in life.

We need, to constantly invest, in improving our competence. Before we can grow professionally, we must be grown personally. The time in our life is limited. It is, upto each one of us, to decide, as to what is the most important thing, to which we should be devoting it. It is not, that I do not attend to routine matters. I pay attention to them, only, after my highest priority, work is over.

Things like shopping, is combined by me, with other tasks, when the departmental stores, or concerned shops fall on my way. The stark reality is that we can not determine our priorities, unless, we resolve, as to what are the highest priorities, both in our life and work.

Then we should make it a point, to make sure, that they find place, not only in our life, but also in our day to day living. The only key, to a successful life, is to live by your priorities. We should always be taking time to truly identify, as to, whether what we are doing is the most important thing in our life. You can make, your own assessment of it, on the scale of 1 to 100 or 0 to 10 and then appraise, everything by it. Apart from the computers and mobile, I still prefer to write on a note book, as to on what I should be spending my time on. This ensures that I do not omit anything vital relevant to my life and work.

Choose which life-priority is the most important thing for you. It should be yours not only the first, but also second, third, and fourth priority in life. A priority gives a direction to our lives.Whatever you do, your life's priorities should be used as a compass, to judge its importance.

A few days, I had three engagements, on one day. I weighed the return from each one of them and cut out, one of a cocktail and engagement, which would have meant spending at least three hours in the evening, apart from the journey time of two hours. I wrote a beautiful letter to the host, explaining the circumstances, which prevented me from attending the programme. Some of them were absolutely true and some were garbled. It is impossible to be totally 100% truthful all the time, as we live in social milieu. Moreover it is not worthwhile to spoil any relationship, with anybody, as long, as it can be maintained with a phone call or a letter.

It is a routine for even unknown people to ring you up, even on your mobile phone, at all odd hours. Earlier, I used to respond, to every phone call, no matter, from where the call emanated. Now I make it point to ignore some calls, as even the best of mobile number does no longer remain a secret.

On the same principle, I make it a point to save the numbers I want to respond to and ignore the rest. My idea behind doing it is to make my count and matter, in the ways, most beneficial to me. It is not that I am being egoistic. It is because, I want to use my time, most constructively and helpfully. I do not feel guilty, for living and working, by own priorities, rather than somebody else's. We can succeed, in our life's mission and goals, only by living and doing what we feel matters most to us, in life.

This is the only way in which you can become a champion. It is not that the champions had everything falling in place or they were luckier than other or had more skills or expertise than an average person or had more money.

Infact the champions had probably faced far greater difficulties or challenges to overcome. Studies after studies have revealed, that it is our attitude which makes us a failure or a success. There is a price tag on any achievement or success. Failures are the ones, who are not willing or do not pay the price of achievement. The thing that can make you great is your tenacity and persistence to keep on striving, even when, facing mountain of obstacles.Even if the champions are facing a slum in their efforts, they keep on going, as against failures and run of the mill individuals, who give up as soon as they face, the first hurdle . It is their attitude, which makes them champions. Each one of us can become a champion, if we follow the postage, which sticks on, till it reaches the destination.

■■■

42

How To Patent Your Success And Make A Place For Yourself In Life And Work?

We need, to take care, of small stuff and minor problems, in our lives, before they become bigger and more complex. It is exactly, like letting your laundry, pile up, unwashed for a week. It will swell to a mountain, leading to the demoralisation for the person who is to launder them.

We are all tempted to use the nearest, open space, for stacking, whether it is the daily mail or newspapers or even our used cup of coffee and tea. I am equally guilty, but occasionally, of putting my things, wherever I can find open area.

Now, I have earmarked a home for every thing I have to use. My effort now is, that, instead of keeping the things randomly, I should keep them, in their earmarked place. This does not take even a minute, but has the great advantage of leaving the place spick and span. A messy place, with papers scattered all over and everywhere, is a huge disincentive to work. This approach, also, has the benefit, of not wasting our time, for finding out, as to where we have kept our belongings and second guessing the same.

It has not only the advantage of decluttering, but also, of tracing the effects, when next required.

You should not, allow yourself, to become a *victim* of the clutter, but learn to move to the role of a *victor*. One way, to motivate yourself, is to discover, as to how, any activity, including decluttering, will further and accelerate, your realising the goals.

After all, the purpose of, doing anything, is to achieve your set goals. No goal can be achieved without working for it. Most of us become victims of starting something and then, not completing the same, for some reason or the other.

We must bear in mind, that no achievement of any goal will magically pop up, without our working for it. Any project, which we might start, has its own challenges, which may not be apparent or clear, when we start our work. Unless, we are flexible and are willing to adjust to the changed circumstances, chances are that we will remain stuck up where we are.

Completing any project entails, proper planning, as well as, both conscious and passionate action. You have to chart out and arrange for the resources, you need or want, for achieving your ambition. Resources and manpower planning is vital for every project. However, no planning can be exhaustive and cover every point.

Nevertheless, it is best to have a starting point and an outline than starting blank. It is just like starting a marathon, where you must have a starting point before you can finish it.

The problem with most people is that they start their most important project, without even a skeletal outline. Infact, a plan of action puts purpose in anything we do. I find that if I start my day without any plan or at least an outline of what I should be doing during the day, I keep on meandering aimlessly. The aimlessness can take the form of putting on the TV, changing channels, phoning up unnecessarily or eating snacks .

As long as you write something about what you should concentrate on, remember that evaluation and upgrading, can always be done later on. It should be done, as far as possible sector wise or point wise or work wise, as may be required, about the task, you are undertaking or have taken up.

In case, any budget is required, this should be provided for , along with a realistic time frame work. Time frame, along with resources are of no use, unless, they are integrated with your schedule and over all life time goals. Ask yourself, whether, whatever you are doing, is what you should be doing to achieve your goals. It might turn out to be a choice between going to a party or sitting all alone and doing your work on a laptop.

Life does not work out, to the last detailed points, we might have wanted. Do not underestimate the time required to complete any task. You have to provide for a buffer time, to meet any unforeseen contingencies or unexpected pressing demands, on your time. Repeated interruptions or attempts to reach your target can lead to the loss of enthusiasm and energy, as well as demoralise us.

Another thing, to be borne in mind is never, to be hung up on unimportant interruptions or trying to be a perfectionist. Once I was discussing the matter of writing any article or a book, with my wife, who had headed the Publications Division of the Government of India. She was its official and a leading publisher. She told me that an important thing to be borne in mind, was never to revise, or polish any writing for more than two times. If you do so, in trying to be a perfectionist, you end up with the first draft.

The ideal is, to do your best, but at the same time, quit being a perfectionist. This is one way, to ensure, a higher success rate, in any thing we do.

Our objective, should be, to complete a project, to the best of our abilities. We should not prevent ourselves, from doing so, because we are aiming at perfection, at all the time, in every aspect.

Except for God, nobody is perfect. For the sake of realising our ambitions, we have to sacrifice a number of claims, on our times, for temporary gratifications. You can adopt your own standards for assessing whether any activity is worth the time, you are spending on. Last month, I had to go for addressing a seminar. I was also due to meet the publisher of my next book, as well as socially meet another friend. I so arranged that after addressing the programme, I met my publisher, immediately , with whom I had fixed a meeting, well in advance. After the meeting, I went for the social get together. This saved me three trips from my house, which would have meant a commuting time of at least six hours, on three days. But by combining all these activities, I would finish them at one go. There was no way, I could have avoided all the three programmes, but a skilful combination of them and that also independently without letting others know, that I was doing so, helped me to save my time.

It is vital, not to allow yourself to be distracted by disruptions, from your focus, of your significant goals, however pressing they may appear to be. This is something, only we can do and nobody else can do for us. Ultimate responsibility for our lives lies on us. ■■■

43

How Our Character Development Can Lead To Personality Development?

The personality of an individual is a combination of characteristics and traits that makes each individual unique. It is, these characteristics, which define a person, as witty, charismatic, charming, intellectual or introvert, extrovert or serious. We change or develop our personality, in response to our environment, perceptions, circumstances, as well as, by the difficulties we overcome. Our personality comprises of different fundamental characteristics and constituents that make up the totality of an individual's whole being.

Every situation can transform our personality. It has direct relationship with our appearances, looks, attitudes, conduct and behaviour. The idea of having a good personality, and in developing, one is to be a winner in life, so that we can attract friends and influence people, both in our professional and social fields.

A good personality, which is tremendously influenced by our character gives us a head start in life. The personality of an individual is not only about physical appearance, or height, weight, social or official stature or complexion. Though physical appearance have their own role and do matter to an extent, there are other important physical characteristics like character, behaviour and attitude, which are basic to any personality.

Personalities have been classified into extrovert—agreeable, conscientious, neurotic, and open to experience. Extroversion reflects outgoing reveals being, sociable, full of energy, enthusiasm, and action-oriented. Introversion, on the other hand, refers to lack of liveliness and energy. Agreeable manifests our different self-interest and personal well-being. Conscientious is evident in individuals who are emotionally reactive and may have gone through or are going through a particular strong negative feeling. Openness to experience is a trait that characterizes people who are creative, imaginative, curious, and intellectuals.Our personality is characterized not just by one aspect of our whole character such as our behaviour or attitude. They are also affected by our patterned thoughts and feelings. Our personality also focuses on how we manage and control our impulses and desires. Conscientious people are intelligent, organized, and persistent.

Personality is like an edifice or a house, which can exist and survive only, when it has a strong foundation. A personality can impress others, only when it has an impressive and a notable basis rooted in unshakeable ethics. Fakes both in life, character as well as in marketing, are short lived. They are of no use in the long term.

Whatever may be claimed, the fact remains, that our best personality traits, are based only, on the solid foundation of our character. For development of our personality, we need to improve our behaviour, communication skills, interpersonal relationships, attitude towards life, values we cherish, as well as our ethical values.

Personality is what makes every individual exceptional, exclusive and inimitable . For bettering our personality, we have to have a desire and determination, as well as identify our goal and how we are going to achieve the same. Above all, we need to dedicate, ourselves to them. We need, to carve out our own path, rather than the path chosen or taken by others, for the simple reason that each one of us, is distinctive and has our special goals.

To enhance your personality, you will need to work hard. It is not something to be done, once in a while and then forgotten. It is something, for which you will have to work constantly. It is for each individual to decide, as to, on what areas, he or she needs to focus, for building up his or her personality.

It is for you to determine and discover , as to in what areas, you need to develop and improve. You can do this, by observing your self attentively, for uncovering, your flaws. You can improve only, if you decide, on the areas, which need this kind of attention.

This is the first step towards becoming a better person and enhancing your personality. Never tell yourself, even in your dreams, that you cannot do so. If you do so, you are only limiting yourself. You have to develop a 'can do' attitude, and believe in yourself and then everything will follow. Your belief that you can make anything happen, which you resolve upon, is the the most vital stepping stone to success. Never even remotely autosuggest to yourself, that you cannot achieve your goal. In other words, don'ts should be out of your life.

Consistency is the key, to attain any ambition. Consistency and character continuously go together. Do not become a slave, to your moods, by telling yourself, that you would do something, vital for your life and personality tomorrow or you are not inclined to do so.

It is a different thing to be busy doing something and not being in a mood to do something. Your mind must know, that it is the master and the moods do not control it. While you cannot have control on your health and well beings, you can always have control on you disposition, feelings and temper.

Practice is vital in achieving excellent results, whether it is in developing your character or for building up your personality. Continuous practice, is the only way to improve in any aspect of our life, precisely like athletes practising every day, on a regular basis, before they can win an Olympic medal. Character and personality development are not easy, as everywhere, you will encounter hindrances and difficulties. It is easier to be tempted to give in than confront and overcome them. Any movement backwards from your goal will pull you down.

There are immense possibilities within each one of us, to develop our personality with strong character. But you have to spot and create them, by utilising your capabilities, your thoughts and your ideals. Building our character and our personality is a personal matter. Nobody else can make us mentally and physically strong and powerful and transform our failure to success.

None can turn a weak, unsuccessful person to a powerful, individual. This is, a 'do-it-ourselves' job. Bear in mind that Character is the light which shines when the sun is down, and all other lights are out. It is that power with which we can win victory even when losing battles. ■■■

44

How To Carve A Niche For Yourselves?

An important aspect of each one of your activity should be to assess whether it is relevant or smart enough for your goals. You have to accept responsibility for your own judgments and of any action, you embark on.

Any purpose in your life, for realisation requires productivity. Whatever you do, must fit your purpose. It should also aid in converting your ideas, into a physical form.

For your Self-Esteem, you must practice Pride, in your commitment, for achieving your own moral perfection. Your chosen values should be always finding a place, in every aspect of your life, on a consistent and a constant basis.

It is a good policy to examine your activities on a regular basis, preferably daily, but not late than on, weekly basis, so as to assess, as to how far, they have been consistent with your goals. What your daily activities should be is for each individual to decide.

Infact daily activities, should always have a relationship with your long and short term goals. I use computer extensively. Print out of the letters and other communications, which are to be sent, are required, for responding to others. The ink cartridge of the printer, had finished its life and instead of sending anybody, I along with my Secretary went to the market, last month, and got the cartridge, so that my urgent letters could be sent to the concerned.

But I made sure, that I combined it, with other shopping so that I did not have to go in the same direction again. We are the captains of our life, and like the sailors sailing on high seas or the pilots flying an aeroplane, we should be able to map or schedule our departure, arrival, precisely as planned, in the blue print of our life.

Once a young sailor asked an old sea Captain, "How do you keep yourself out of that predicament, if you are caught between a violent storm and a dangerous reef and still stay, on a profitable course?"

Replied the Captain, "How you do that, is to study and integrate, into your being, a philosophy, for living and working, so that, in the first place, you do not get into that situation?"

Infact, we do not need the blue print not only for our full life but for every day of our life. It does not take more than 10 minutes to do so, day after day. It is upto, each one of us, to decide, whether to prepare it, before sleeping, in the night, or just before starting the day. While I personally do it, every night, at the same time, I go on adding the items, that occur to me, even at midnight. Then I select the most important one, and focus on principal and key tasks to be done first, before taking up, other lesser important assignments.

The normal tendency is to first take up the easier jobs and not the most important one. Unless this is reversed, we will end our day, feeling empty, and dissatisfied. We should not allow ourselves to be side tracked, by minor crises and interruptions . At the end of the day, it is the amount of action, you put into the day, doing your vital chores, which will determine your success or failure.

You cannot stretch a 24 hour day to 25 or 30 hours. But you can, ruthlessly cut out, all activities, which come in the way of your goals. I, on my part, prefer to dispose off most of the visitors on telephone, rather than meeting them, I tell them politely, that it would take half of their day, in coming to Dwarka, to see me, as well as the inconvenience of travelling so far off. I suggest to them, to send me an email or a letter and I would get back to them. I do so and as a matter of principle, every communication is replied, unless, it is something scurrilous or frivolous or scandalous.

This way, I can protect my time, as well as, help others, to save their time. Truthfully, I am more concerned, with saving my own time than anything else. I keep up my promise by either telephoning or emailing, if I cannot accept any engagement or my Secretary does it on my behalf. Even if I go for a dinner or for any another appointment, I tell my host, the amount of time, I would spend, which rarely exceeds 45 to 60 minutes for any activity.

Another important thing to be done, is to take time to expand your knowledge. I do it almost everyday, by keeping myself updated, in the fields relating to my work, as well as to motivate myself. Even during my morning walk, to stimulate myself, I listen to good reading on my digital recorders which have at least 200 hours of recording limit and some have even much more.

At the end of the day, I introspect and question myself, as to , I have performed during the day and whether there is anything, I could have done better. I also ask myself, whether I have wasted any of my time, on the activities, which were of insignificance or zero return to me.

Another thing, which I always, bear in mind that I am a human being and liable to be tired physically. I just take rest to recuperate my energy level. A few minutes rest freshens me and I can work upto my highest level of energy. I make no bones, about taking rest and I make no claim, that I can live or work without adequate rest, to the peak of my efficiency. I have always done so, in my nearly 37 years of Government service. The rest time is sacrosanct for me and except for the Prime Minister of the country, when I was the Director of the CBI, I did not permit anybody to disturb me, for the rest period of 20 minutes after lunch.

This is equally applicable to all human beings, whether they admit it or not. To overcome challenges and for scaling new heights, it is upto us, to devise our own individualised methods and treat them as stepping stones, rather than stumbling blocks. It is entirely upto each one of us, as to how we view them. There are no routes or short cuts to the quality of life, we wish to have. ■■■

45

How To Protect Your Interests and Time?

I will admit it frankly that if somebody either a friend or an acquaintance or even a total stranger makes a request to me for anything, I would prefer to say 'Yes'. This approach, is the result of my feeling that I do not want to disappoint anybody. Even if, I can not say 'No', I would like go to the maximum extent to help. This is because I want to build bridges and not burn them. My effort is not to disappoint anybody to the extent I can, so that my relationships with others is not jeopardised. This is probably which most people feel.

While saying — 'Yes', is the easiest thing, it is not always the best response and reply, all the time. When we say 'Yes', to something or a person, we are saying No to something else, including ourselves. Just like saying "No", like saying "Yes" has several implication.

For example, by saying 'Yes' to seeing a movie, with your friends, when you have other pressing work, or you are to prepare yourself for the final examination, you are saying 'No' to yourself. Similarly, when you work late to complete a job, by sitting late in your office or work place, you are saying 'No' to your social life and to your family time. By participating in one set of activities, you are denying yourself another set of actions.

Our effort should be to grow and to be our best self. We should not engage in the things, which do not support our dreams and our passions. You should say No to the people or friendships or other relations which hold you back. You do not have to put up with insults or humiliations from others for the sake of not offending them. If some relationships are not compatible with your requisites, it is better to part and pursue different paths. This way, you will not be coming in the way of each other.

If something does not fit in with your purpose , it is best to say No to it, as well as to the things, which are of no importance and significance to your life. You should not participate in inconsequential and trivial activities, which do not add value to your life and which are a waste of time. Your activities should be, in alignment with your aspirations. If something, is not going to help you, in the realisation of your ambition, you should not invest your time and energy into them. It has to be borne in mind, that nothing can be achieved, by only sitting on a chair, and contemplating that how good life it would be, after you have realised your goal. You have to go and make it happen.

The path of attaining your objectives, requires your saying No to many more things, on a regular basis, rather than saying, one time 'No'. A good policy would be, to have a catalogue for one month, starting from today, to the things, you have said 'Yes' or 'No'. At the end of the month, you would have a clear picture, as to, to what you have said, Yes, when in fact, it would have been better to say 'No'. You do not have to say ' Yes' to the people, who do not appreciate, or respect you, or to the activities, which prima facie, you do not relish and in reality are a waste of time.

I had an invitation to visit Bangalore to attend a wedding last month. The host had sent a club class, air ticket and a confirmed reservation in a Five Star Hotel. I had met the host only once, and spoken to him twice on phone. It would have been a waste of three days and meet the people I hardly knew or was not likely to meet again. I just sent a cheque with a polite letter, and a suitable excuse, as to why I was not able to attend the wedding. Most of the time, the hosts of any function, want a few photographs, to show that he knows the big wigs, to impress others. This is what socialisation has come to pass these days.

To the extent possible, I make it a point not to spend more than 45 minutes in any socialisation or other similar programme. After my part of meeting the host or getting photographs is over, I leave the place. To any invitation extended to me, I tell the host in advance, as to how much time, I can spend. My idea, behind all this, is to save time, to do the things I want to do and to spend time, on the dreams and goals, I want to achieve.

If you are not concerned or bothered about your goals and dreams, be sure nobody else would be bothered about them. Saying Yes to yourself and no to Non essentials, is an ongoing exercise. It is not a one time endeavour. Whenever, you get a request, critically examine, as to what will be the result of your saying 'Yes', or 'No', along with the long term implications of gains and losses. Remember, that it is, within the powers, of each one of us, to say No to something, which does not suit your interests, and affects in your engaging in the activities, relevant to your interests. This is the only way to live your life to the fullest and to protect your interests and time. ■■■

46

How to Let By Gones, Be By Gones?

Change is something, which is inevitable. Whether, we like it not, or wish it or not, it is bound to come. Those leaders, who do not change with the times, cease to be leaders or the drivers of change. A closed mind, is the biggest obstacles to any change. It is not relevant only to the leaders, but also to the people working with them, as well as to each one of us. It is a truism, that those, who do not change, with the changing times, are left behind. Fortune, not only favours the brave, but also those, who are prepared for it, as well as those who are ready for the change.

Before the manual type-writers were invented, all reports including the Government orders, used to be hand written. Printing press and type-writers brought a kind of revolution, in the early part of 19th and 20th Century. Electric and electronic type - writers, further refined the art of written communication. Now the type-writers are a passé and except for a few pieces with some people, they can only be found in museums. With the arrival of computers and laptops, as well as Emails, at the lightening speed, not only the methods of working have changed, but the pace as well, as expectation of the promptest reports. I travelled to USA at the request of an organisation. Their air ticket was with me, within seconds, after I had emailed my passport to them.

Not only we have to change, as well, but also to provide opportunities to those working with us, not only to be well trained, but also to assimilate and imbibe the expertise, as well as, acquire competence. This is the only way to be a winner in the present competing environments. Whatever be our profession or work, we should be proactive to change.

I admit that most of us, including myself, have resisted the change, on the ground that the existing practices and approach is good enough for our work. At one time, I myself refused to move from the type-writer to the computer age. But when the advantages were brought home to me, I became the greatest protagonists of the computers. I have realised, that if you want advancement, and go ahead, you have to accept that change is inescapable.

Only, as drivers of the change, we can truly, empower ourselves, and obtain outstanding results. The only place, where there is no change, for the human beings, is the graveyard. Not changing with the situation and new requirements, amounts to getting stale and lethargic, like the stagnant water. There are a few things, we do not like, either in the world or in the others, or even in ourselves.

If we cannot do anything to change them, then for our own equanimity and composure, we should transform our thinking about them. It is not obligatory to change, if you do not want to survive in a competitive world. We must accept that both good and bad situations are bound to change, in a cyclical manner.

What we become in life, is the price we have paid, to reach where we are or want to be. Another thing, to be borne in mind is, that by changing our thoughts, we can change our world. Our life is what our thoughts make it. The trees or people, who survive, are those, who adjust with the times, gales and are most responsive to change. You must be dissatisfied with the present, to change for the better. The only way, to improve in life, is to keep on adding, walking and advancing. Every beginning, is the consequence of something we have done or not done. It is also the beginning, of some thing new.

There is a nice prayer, on change, which I have read quite often. It says some thing like this that God grant me the serenity to accept the things, and people I cannot change, the courage to change, whatever I can and the wisdom to know the difference. Any change, in our style or approach, to rectify the past mistakes, gives us almost a second chance, to rectify any given situation. Our future depends on us, as no wise or a brave man, gives a chance to the train of future, to run over him.

Nothing stays all the time as as same and unchanged, as two men, never judge the same thing as identically. Even the opinions of the same man changes at different times and in diverse situations. Not only we have to change with the times, but also apply new innovations. When things worst, they have to be altered accordingly. A good approach in life is find happiness, in whatever we have to do or in whatever we are doing. We should not make a career of being unhappy, because people and circumstances change. Whining, carping and cribbing does not lead to any results, except being miserable, gloomy and dismayed.

Once I sought help from a close friend of mine, for a very small matter, which was in his power. He put me off, with a lecture, as to how, it was not, in my interest, to have a particular matter done, in my favour. I had done a lot for him and had known him for over five decades. I felt upset, and did not speak to him for 10 years, till he invited me, for his son's wedding. By that time the hurtful behaviour was forgotten. When we met again, I had forgotten my hurt and incident. I met him warmly, as if nothing, unpalatable had happened between us.

Our emotions are transient and we should not become their slaves. Our effort should be, to have the right chemistry with men and matters. Every day, remind yourself , of the blessings, with which you are gifted, like good health, a good position in life, a loving family, good place to live in and a few affectionate friends and relatives.

I went for a wedding to another friend's place. There were over a hundred guests and with great difficulty, I could spot only two to whom I could speak, including a class fellow whom I was meeting after 50 years. I enjoyed talking to him and then after a decent interval left the party, after thanking the host. It does not pay, to make yourself miserable, more than you can tolerate, for the sake of pleasing others. The idea of any activity, you indulge in, is to find happiness. Happiness basically is a by product, of whatever we do. It is not something, you can demand from life or from others. But you have to work for it. ■■■

47

How to live Life On Your Own Terms Magnificently?

No body and nothing in the world is perfect. If everybody or everything in the universe was perfect, there would be no need for improvement and upgradation. We all realise that things or our circumstances could be better. At the same time, it is upto each one of us, to make our life, work and circumstances better. Nobody else is going to do it for us.

The critical part of our life, is to decide, what is most important and necessary, both for our work, our family and our life. You have to plan for it and decide as to what you are going to do, about it. Even if you have done something for a number of year, the ideal approach, is to plan for it. I have travelled hundreds of times out of Delhi, but I make sure in advance, that I have packed everything I want when I am out of house. This includes not only my clothings but also the tickets for travelling, reading material my laptop, sufficient cash and my cheque books.

Another vital point is to say no to things you do not really want to do or what are not crucial to your scheme of things. You must say, yes only to those things, which are most important and matter critically to your life. If you do not like, an event or the people who will be present at any programme or occasion, there, whom you do not want to meet or whom you do not like it is best to politely regret and say "No, Thank You."

If you are clear, as to what you want to do and what you do not want to do, it will be easier, for you to make a decision as to what to accept and to what, to say No. You have to have workable options. But at the same time, you must choose your battles wisely. If there is a choice of winning a battle, but losing a war, you should rather loose a battle and win a war. In other words, calculate the cost benefit ratio of any action, before you decide, to take it or not take it.

You should always go in for a workable option, with best and unambiguous reasons. By same token, if you get a No from others, you must appreciate their position, as they, might be facing similar problems and difficulties, as you might have had .

Bear in mind that you can only control your response and not the response or reactions of others. Identify the things, you can control and take action accordingly, in your best interests. It is also a fact, that there are, a far greater number of things, circumstances and people about whom, we can do very little, or almost nothing. Any resistance, to these truths of life, would not only be futile, but make us gloomy and disheartened.

Despite the glaring reality , that we cannot do anything, about a few things, like the death of a loved one, we still resist change, despite the evidence, that it has already occurred. In this way, we loose a lot of time and energy in doing so. As an alternative, we should learn, as to what has happened and what experience, we can learn from it. The solution to any bumpy and vicious problem, lies within us, through a powerful self reflection, calmness and patience.

It is true, that several life situations, like a difficult spouse, or a dishonest boss or an employee or a shirking worker, poses all kinds of challenges to us, frequently. It is easier, to give in and accept defeat. If you persist and are unruffled and are level-headed, you will get an appropriate answer, to question as to "what should I do?" Do not be reluctant, to ask for help from others, if you feel that it would be and handy and useful. Each one of us, has reached where we are, by solely pulling ourselves, to the top, from our own bootstraps. We have reached the present situation, because some body bent down and helped us. Despite being extremely tight on budget, but for the foresight, initiative of my parents, I would not, have been to acquire the education, which I did and made it to the Indian Police Service. But, after a limit the basic contribution of studying hard was mine. Fundamentally, and essentially, if you ever need a helping hand, you would find at the end of your arm. Look up and not down. Look forward and not back. Look out and not in, should be our chief approach in life. ■■■

48

How To Deal With Bullies?

We all have had a chance and our share of bullies in our lives, whether they come in the form of our colleagues, neighbour, friends or even bosses. Bullies rely on criticisms and allegations, which are ostensibly about you or your performance and which rarely contain a grain (but only a grain) of truth. They are , not generally about you, or your best performance. Do not be fooled, into believing the criticisms and allegations have any validity. They do not have any.

The purpose of the bully's criticism is to control men, events and what is already being done well . It has nothing to do, with anybody's performance improvement. Bullying can be open or behind closed doors. First of all, recognise, as to, what is happening. The bully has an ego problem, which he is projecting on to you.

Criticisms and false allegations, are the weapons, in the armoury of the bully. Many may say, that they are the weaknesses or shortcomings or failings or a sign, of incompetence of the bullies. The bullies objective is to embarrass or shame or make you feel guilty. It is his tactics of control and silencing his victims. Bullies generally, use deception, amoral behaviour and indulge in abuse of power. The bully is devious, deceptive, evasive and manipulative and he also cheats.

Find out as to what you can do about bullying. Bullies in work place or for that matter, in educational institutions, use victimising as a strategy on people, they perceive to be, weaker and smaller. They can be, outright, both abusive and violent. Regardless of the type you have to deal, with them, for the sake of maintaining your peace of mind. A bully can descend, to the lowest level to show you down and prove to others that he is a superior being.

I myself had an experience of bullying interfering with my working , bordering on the breach of peace. A call to the police for necessary action deflated him totally. Of course to save his face in front of fellow bullies, he put up a brave face and sent a representation, against me to the people working under me. A bully will go as far, as you permit him. A bully's mainstay is getting personal and attacking you with a view to demoralise you.

A bully should be made aware, that his actions, conduct and manners, are unacceptable. You do not have to become aggressive, but convey to him, that he must stop his mischief. You must take care not to stoop to the level of the bullies. You must make it clear to him that his behaviour is intolerable . You can tell him in plain language, that you do not like his conduct. You can be specific, about what has offended you. You must be clear in your mind that you are under no obligation to accept any toxic activities.

If the bullying does not stop, you are within your rights in complaining to the appropriate authorities. It would be best to do so in writing. This can include, complaining to his boss or if he has violated any laws, to the appropriate legal authorities. A bully is normally arrogant. He thinks that he is always right, and has the best answers to all official and life's problems. He believes that he is better than others. But truly, this is only a mask to cover his inner emptiness and inferiority complex.

Bullying and arrogant behaviour is the result of feeling neglected and not being given any central place in any consultation or work with which he may not even be remotely concerned. This is the bully's way for getting all the attention he wants to attract, so that others may regard him as a man of high intellect or intelligence.

Dealing with an arrogant person may require different approaches. Some adopt the approach of ignoring a bully, others, of confronting him and still others of avoiding him. It is something which will depend on the circumstances of a given case. But one thing is certain, that you have to stop such a behaviour, for your own equanimity and serenity. Have either, no dealings, with a bully, or if it is inescapable, then keep the contact to the minimum. Generally keep him at two arms length, at all times.

While dealing with the adverse qualities of others, you should just be yourself. Do not show any feelings of superiority or look down on others and give an impression that you are superior to others. Stay true to yourself and do not lower your standards or values.

Bullies like to play the game that they are superior to others. They also like to belittle others, to cover their own fears and shortcomings. Do not fall into their traps and play the game as they do. Bear in mind that bullies like knocking other people down both intellectually and morally. It is for the simple reason, that the bullies feel that not only they have all the knowledge and information, but they have a monopoly on the right answers.

Whatever be the circumstances, your aim should be, to take the high road and give your best to the world. You do not have to feel intimidated by the arrogant bullies. The answer to dealing with them is to be assertive and remain level-headedness.Look at the things in the proper perspective.You do not haveto match their rudeness with rudeness. A bully does not realise that he is not the centre of the universe, as there are other people in the world. You have to deal with the bullies in a self confident, self assured and polite manner.It is his self perceived self importance, which will lead to his down fall and his hurting himself.But you have to be on your guard against such people all the time.

■■■

49

How to Deal With Self Pity?

According to, Wikipedia, "Self-pity or "feeling sorry for oneself" is the psychological state of mind of an individual in perceived adverse situations who has not accepted the situation and does not have the confidence nor ability to cope with it. It is characterized by a person's belief that he or she is the victim of events and is therefore deserving of condolence.

Self-pity is generally regarded, as a negative emotion, in that it does not generally help deal with adverse situations. However, in a social context, it may result in either, the offering of sympathy or advice. Self-pity may be considered normal, and in certain circumstances healthy, so long as it is transitory and leads to either acceptance or a determination to change the situation.

Whenever we face a tough situation, or which we perceive is unfair, then we tend to, indulge in self pity and tell ourselves that we do not deserve it. In other words, we deliberately, make ourselves victims of self pity. Self pity can also be called as modern cowardice. It also arises from the supposition, that we are neither fully understood nor fully appreciated. Infact, self pity is one of the most destructive emotions. As it arises in individuals, it is for such individuals, to make sure, that he or she does not become a victim of this most devastating feeling.

You may be poor, but that is no reason to indulge in self pity. The answer to such circumstances, is to get out of the rut of poverty by taking action, working harder and improving your qualifications, so that you can get a higher paying job. The cure for self gloominess or perverse sentiment, is not to let them control you, or share your awful condition with others, as well as, change your scene and do something about such obsession.

Self pity is one of our worst enemies and to yield to it, is to loose, all hope and self confidence. To feel sorry for yourself, is one of the most disintegrating, destructive and corrosive thing, anybody can do, to himself. It fogs our vision. Everybody has some hindrance or load. But at the same time, each person feels that his is the heaviest.

What poison is to food, self pity is to our life and existence. The reverse of faith is the self pity. It is simply being sorry for one self for any given set of circumstances. It affects the quality of our life, as it demoralises us. We all have some problems, as long as we live. But at the same time, imposing suffering and self pity on ourselves is optional.

We have to safeguard our own interest and not assume or presume that we are unfortunate or the object of self pity. If we do not have all the good things in life, we should assess the blessings we have and others do not have. Instead of comparing ourselves with millionaires and billionaires, let us bear in mind, that even as per the Government figures, 27 crore Indians have an income of Rs. 20 per day. This itself should be enough to convince most people as to how, fortunate they are, against the rest of our countrymen.

It is not to say that we should not strive to better our lives, careers and prospectuses. It is only to emphasise, that self pity for such people is not only a sin against man but also against God. It is open to each one of us not to treat any thing as a hard luck. Even if you feel dishonoured or discredited unjustly, you do not have to acknowledge it. What is born is bound to perish, but we should make sure that we end our life journey not whining, but gloriously.

My parents migrated from the areas which form Pakistan now, in 1947, with myself and my two sisters. I never saw my late father, Mahant Kartar Singh, blaming bad luck or God. He would always tell me to pray that " God give me the strength to accept all situations, with grace and peace of mind".

There were times, when having left behind in Pakistan, more than two thousand acres land , he cut grass and sold it. I grazed cattle, and merrily bathed buffaloes and other animals in the canal, so that I could also take bath there. I never saw my late father grumbling or cursing anybody. Instead of despairing he always tried to find a way out. He used to tell me that if you are willing to accept the good, you must also be willing to accept the bad.

It is not the burden in our life, which breaks our back, but the way, we carry it. We must bear in mind, never to communicate our misery to others, as it is a communicable disease. Self pity is a very destructive emotion, a kind of non-pharmaceutical narcotics. Infact, self pitying leads to people in wallowing in their own desolation and gloom.

Instead of doing something to get out of such situations, a self pitying man or a woman delights in a perverse way in his suffering, that separates the victim from reality. Self pity is a sign of insecurity. We should view self pity as our own self problem. The remedy for this is to take action to rectify the situation. It is like, not liking a habit and then taking steps to change it or if you do not like a dress, simply change it. An effort has to be made to think positive for ourselves. You have to go out of the way, to cultivate friends, being nice and liking people. It takes a little effort. But once you start, you will find it easy to excise self pitying feeling, out of your life. ■■■

50

How To Lead A Meaningful and Excuse-Free life?

Every generation, likes to make, its own mistakes, before it realises, that it would have been better to learn, from other's experience. Even the experience of others is of no relevance as we go ahead in life. Each situation, we confront, is different and so the reaction of the people to the same set of circumstances, can vary.

The problem, of most people, is that, they think that their given approach, to any given situation, is the best. No life is mistake proof. What may seem alright in one setting , may not be relevant in others. These days, all facilities, like electricity or electric fans or Air conditioners, are taken for granted. As a student, in the early years of Indian Independence, the only way to study, in the night, was by kerosene lantern or kerosene table lamp.

Not many people had stoves of kerosene for preparing their meals. Nobody had heard of the cooking gas. But, human nature is such that it has been lapped up now. It was a period, when even the cycles were scarce. Most of the time, as a student even till my graduation, I would walk down, to the school or the college from my hostel or even carry my luggage for three kilometres from the Railway

Station to save 2 Annas or equivalent of present 12 Paisas of one Rupee.

As the money was scarce, my late father could afford a cycle for me, after I had graduated. The fact remains, that either you can accept a situation and smile and bear it with a grin, or if it is patent injustice, then do something about it. How we treat and take, a given state of affairs, depends, on each one of us. It is upto, each one of us, to make the hardest thing easier, as truly, nothing is impossible in life. It is again open to us to be scared by barriers in our way to success or to treat them as hurdles, which can be overcome by making a little more effort.

Nobody is interested in failures and whatever excuses, you proffer, will not interest anybody. Incidentally nobody has succeeded in life, through making excuses. As a substitute, for making excuses, we should make good and spend the same time, in attaining our cherished objectives.

We may have our own problems of health, or work or with our colleagues or subordinates or at home or with spouses. Excuses are, one way, of putting things off. Ultimately, our life is our own and no excuses or apologies are good enough to justify about our unsatisfactory, present or future position.

The only way, to forge ahead, is to hold yourself accountable, for a higher standard, than what other expect from you. We should not use sloth and pessimism, as an excuse for the difficulties, which come in the way of achieving our purpose. Any triumph, is a story of obstacles overcome and excuses not used. The same exertion, is required, in succeeding , as is required, for manufacturing excuses, as to why you did not succeed.

There is a difference, between interest and commitment. You have to be committed, to do something, worthwhile, and you do not rest till you have accomplished it. A casual interest, does not get you the same results. When you are committed to something, you are not interested in accepting excuses, either from yourself or from others. You are not satisfied till you get the results. Almost all failures, come from people who have the habit of putting forth excuses.

The law of cause and effect is as absolute and undeviating in every sphere of life. A competent doctor or a management expert, or an administrator is not a matter of accident, or a chance. It is the outcome of a continued focused effort, unremitting dedication and hard work. It is an enduring and unalterable truth, which nobody can change, that every infraction of the Law of Cause and Effect carries its consequences with it. It is impossible to dodge the cause and effect, which are, as inextricably linked, as the seed and its fruit.

We need, to put away aimlessness, with the sole objective, of thinking and working to a purpose. Our thoughts, deeds and words are like the boomerangs, which return to us, duly transformed into our actions or reaction. Success, happiness or punishment, is simply a consequence and result of our actions and thoughts. The present is the cause of our past and on what we have laid emphasis.

Higher marks in studies, which is again the result of hard work, means better and higher paying jobs and recognition in society or appreciation , from our peers or friends or our known circle of people. It is a wise policy to direct our anger, towards problems and not people.

Our force should be directed to for finding answers to any problem, rather than discovering newer and newer excuses, for not succeeding in any venture. Little effort means little results and higher effort results in higher results.

There are no rewards, without work and some element of risk, which is a clear manifestation of the law of cause and effect. If we like people, people will like us. Even if we face, what we may call insurmountable obstacles, a sunny disposition will make trifles of them. We must bear in mind that mostly, we are not disturbed, by things or the people, but by the view, we take of them. We suffer more, from anger and grief, than those very things, over which we are angry or grieved. Bear in mind, that those who wish to sing, always find a song. Says a Chinese proverb :

'Keep a green tree in your heart and perhaps a singing bird will come.'

■■■